SKIN ART TATTOOS

COLORING BOOK

BROOKS BROTHERZ

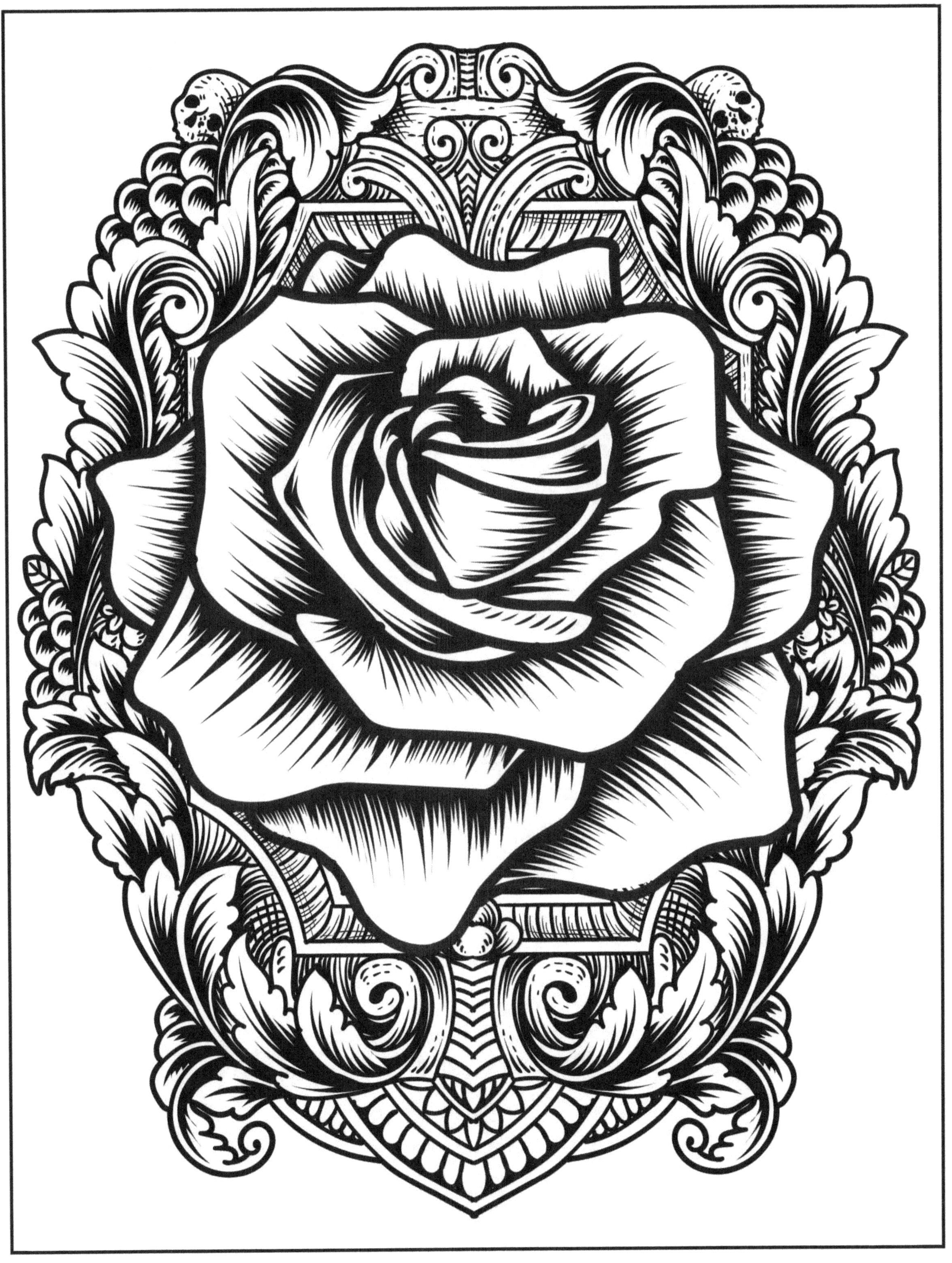

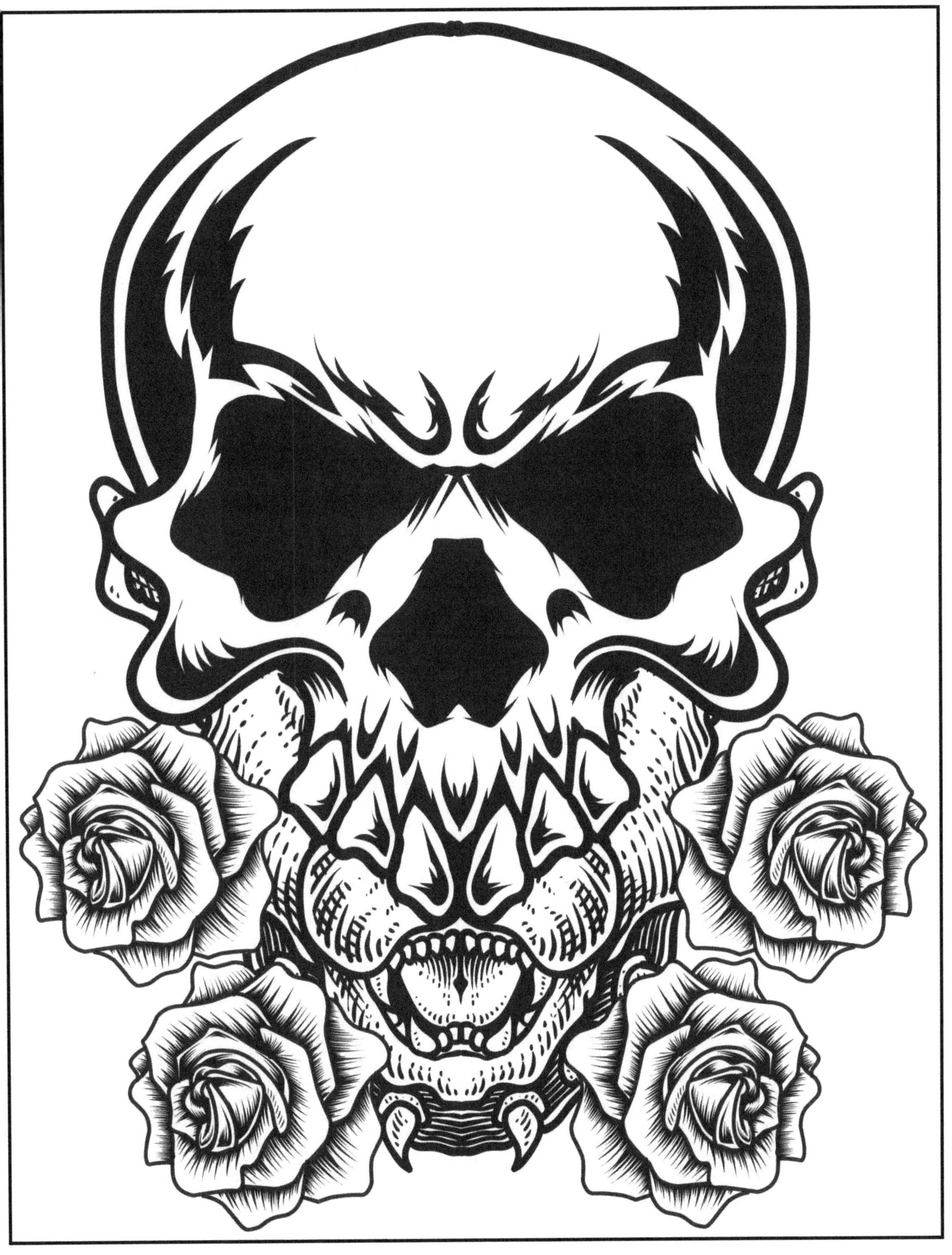

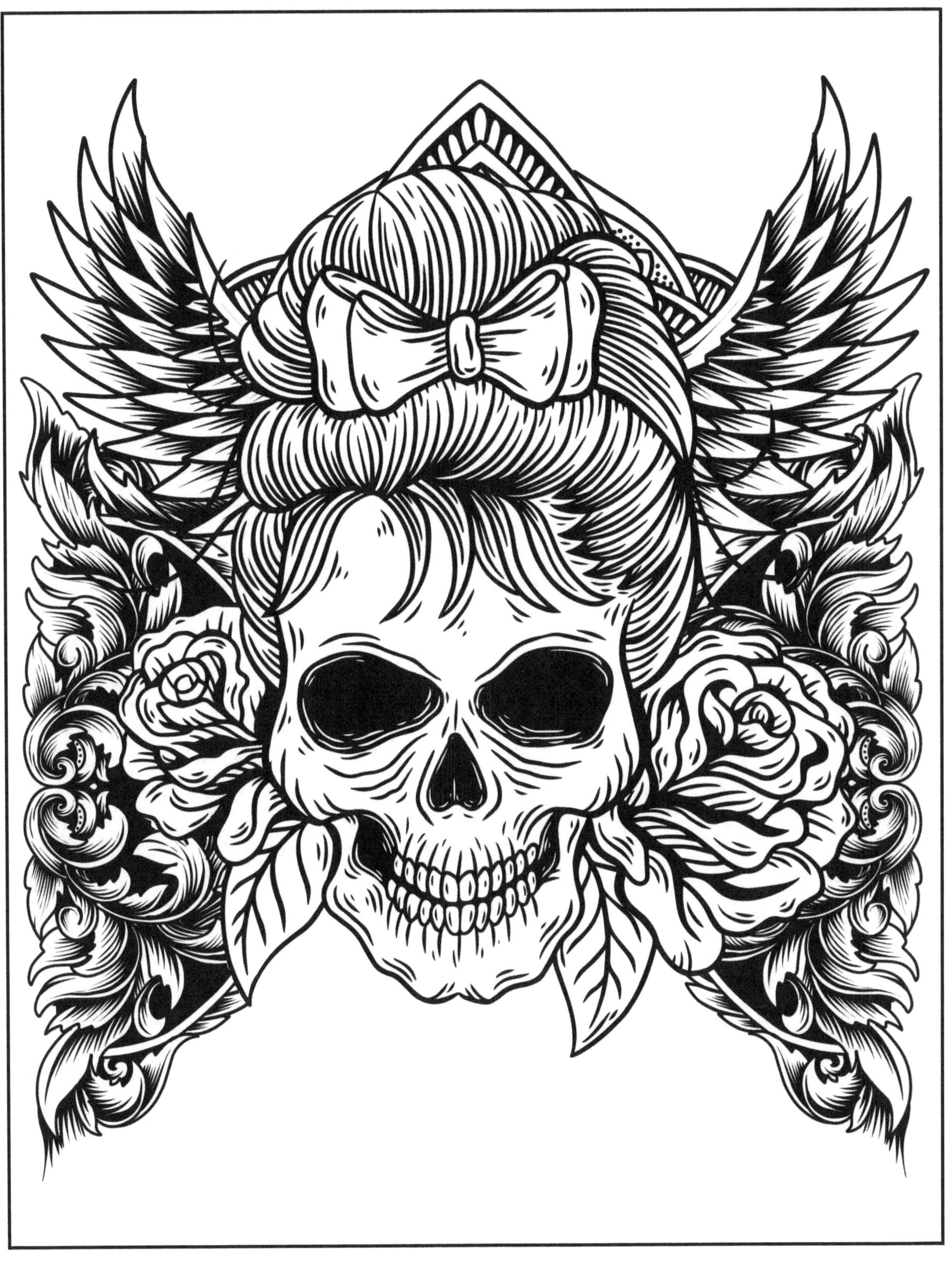

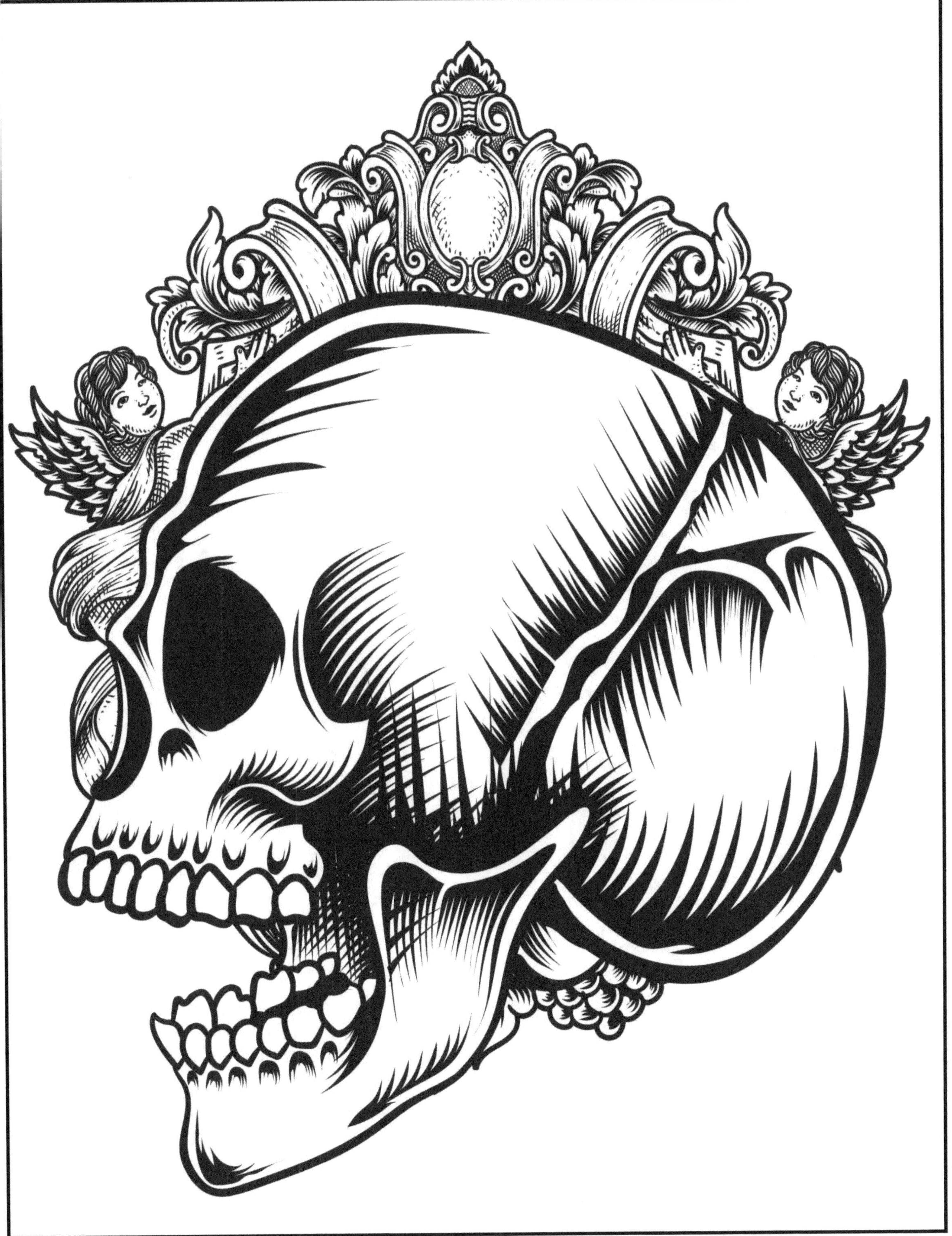

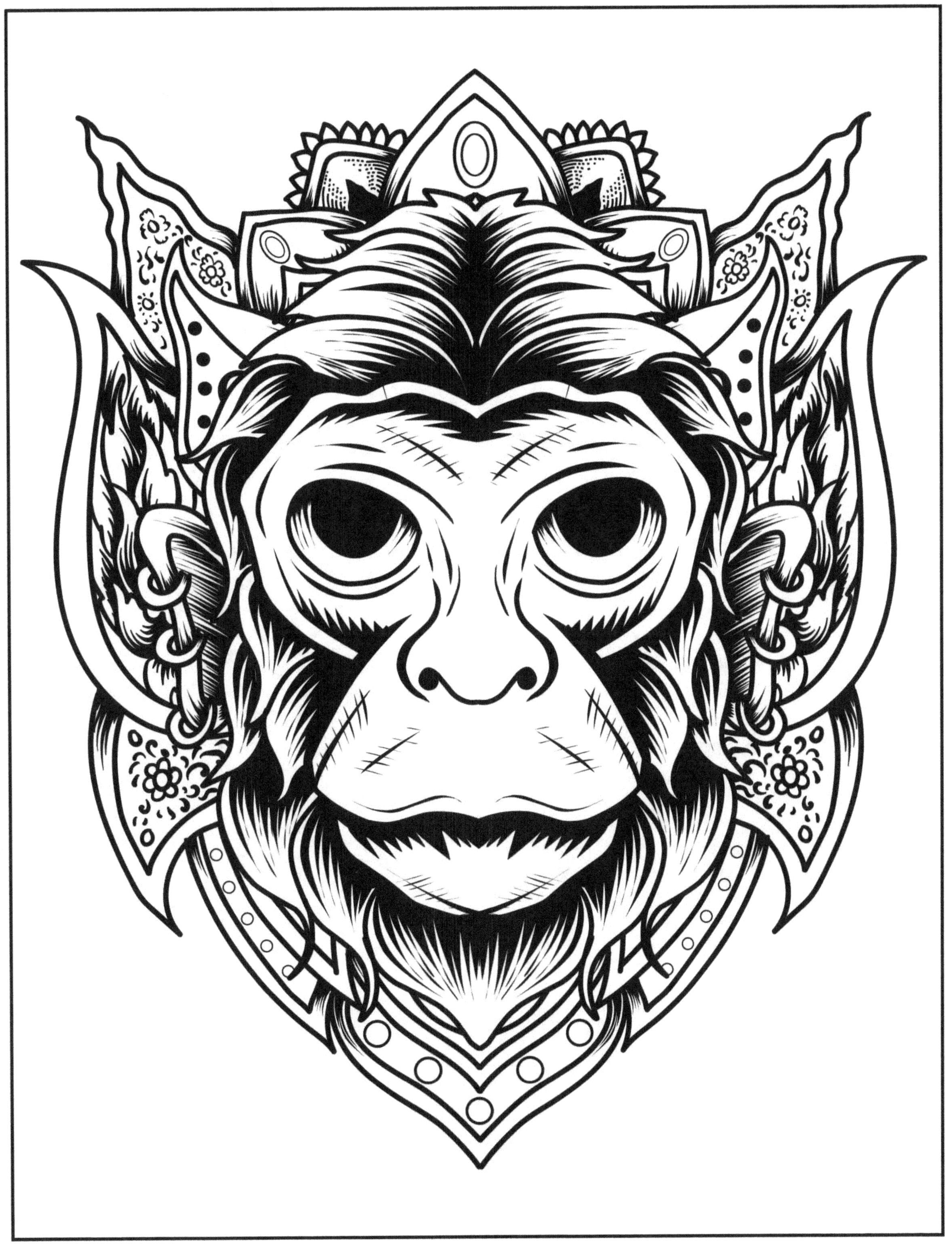

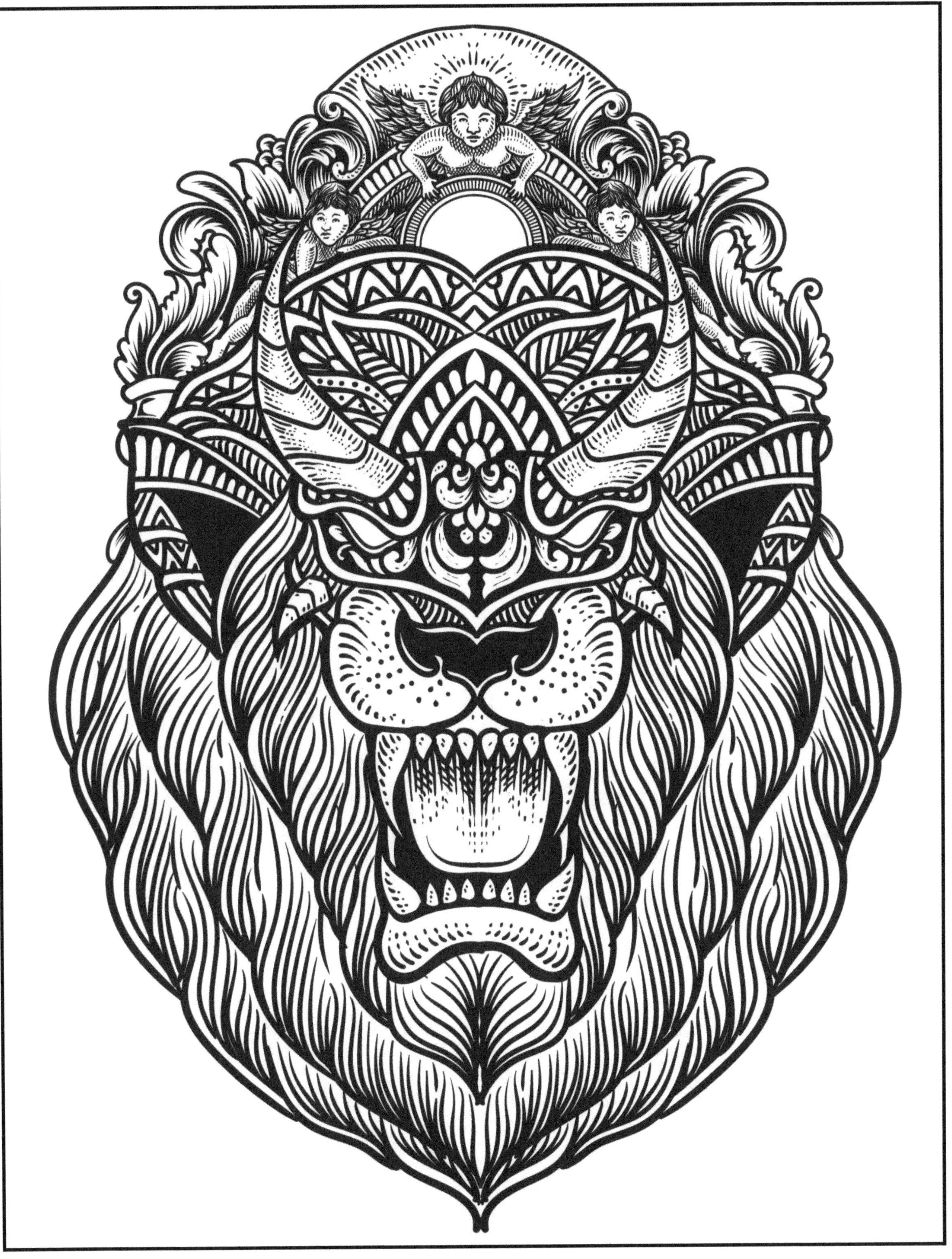

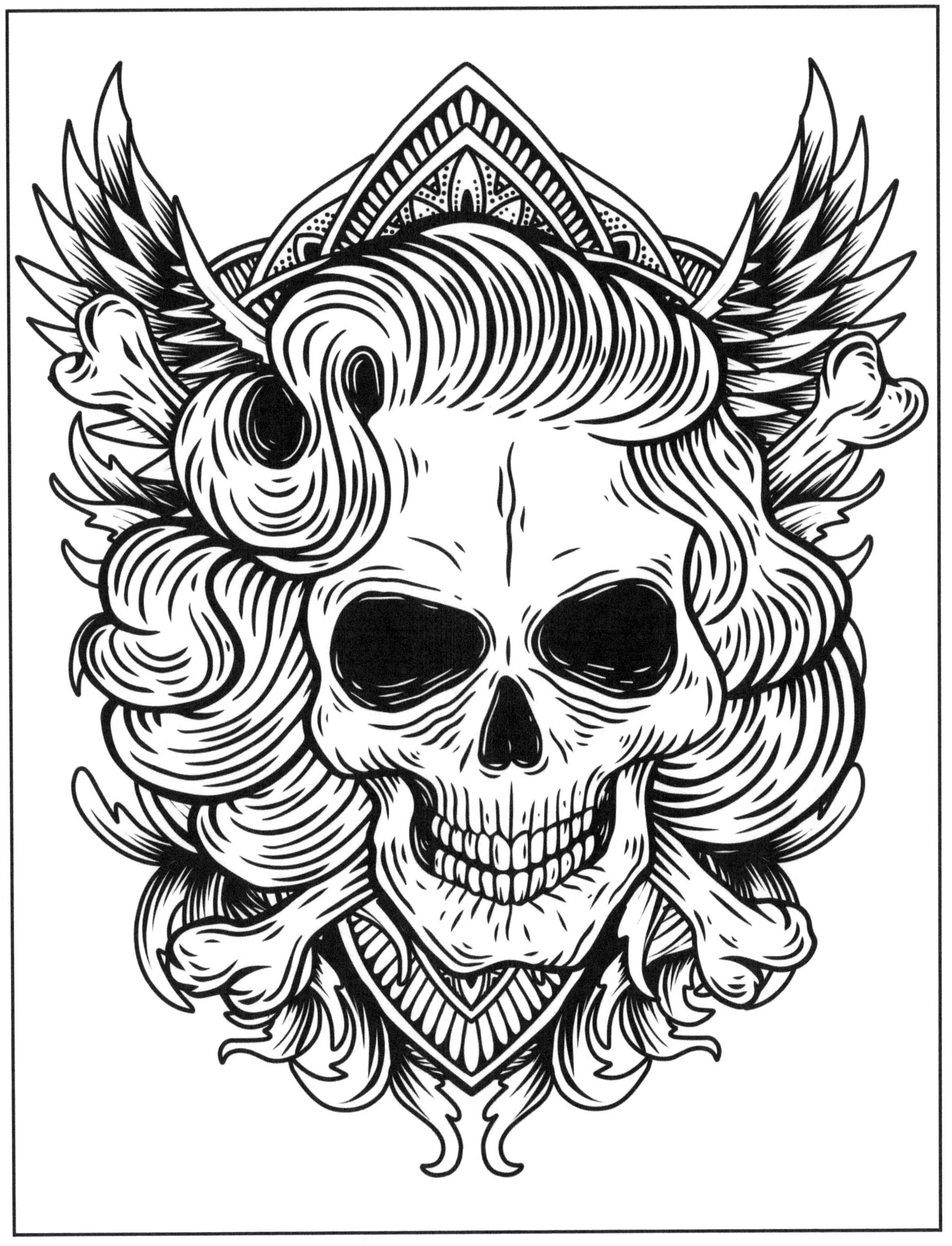

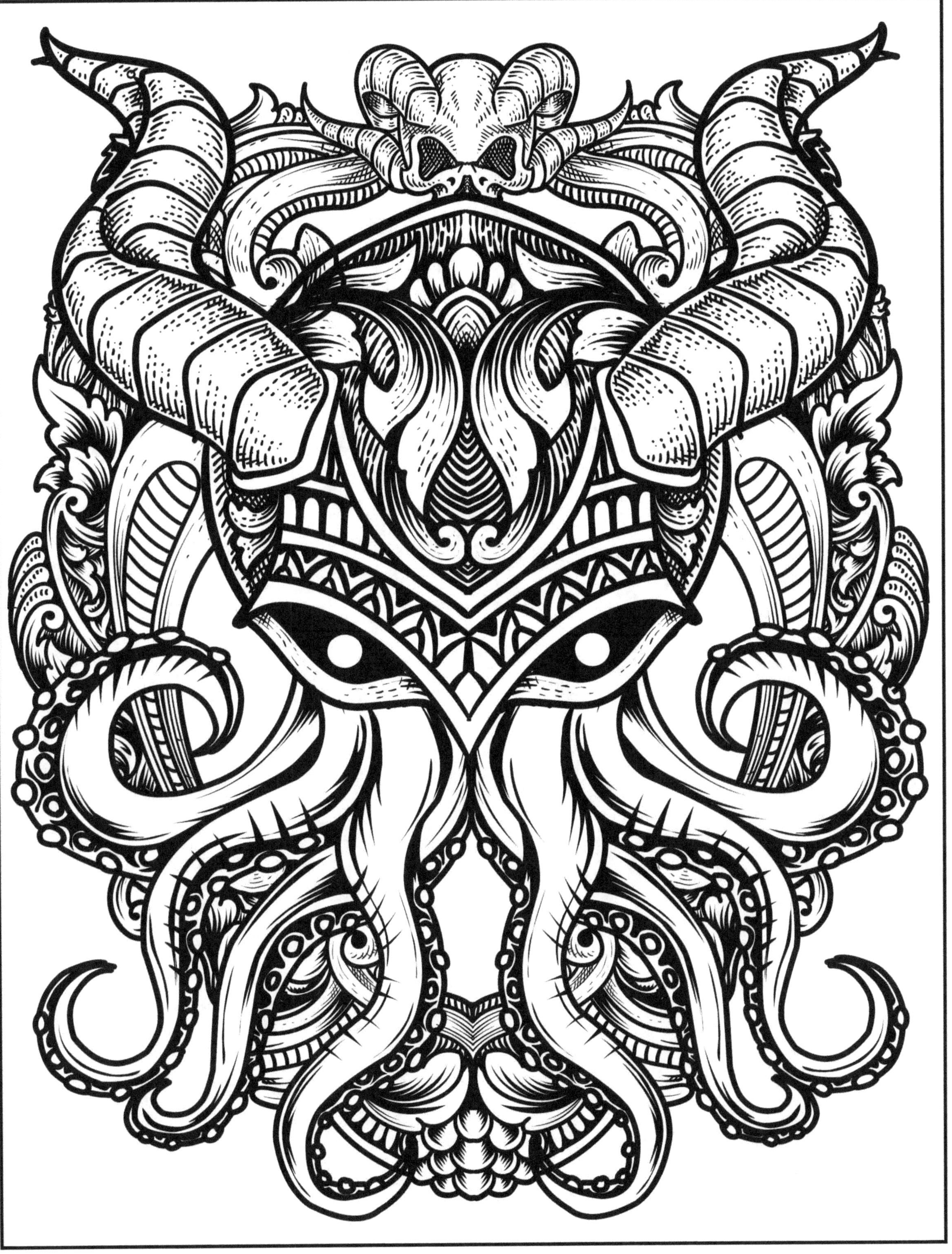

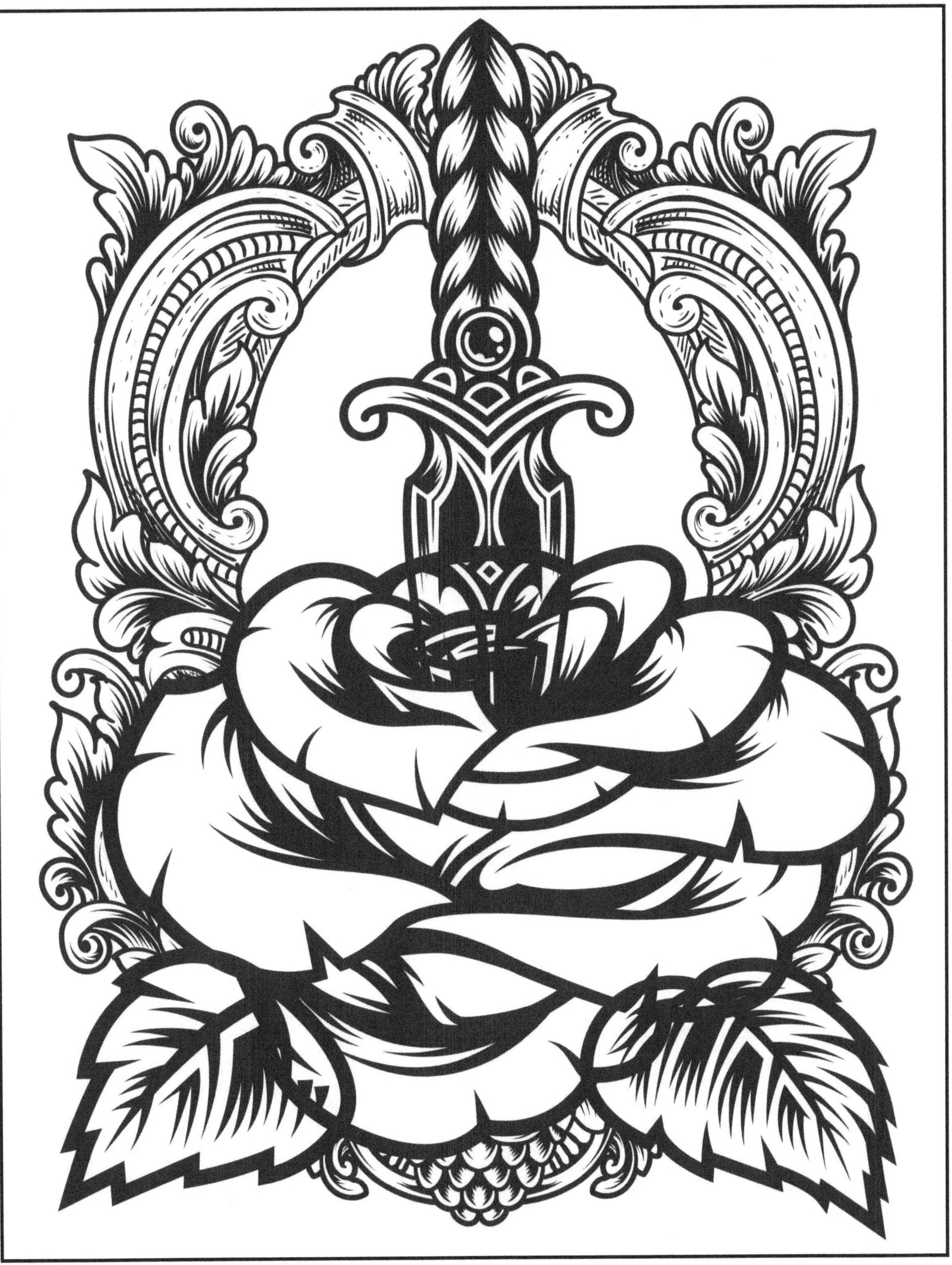

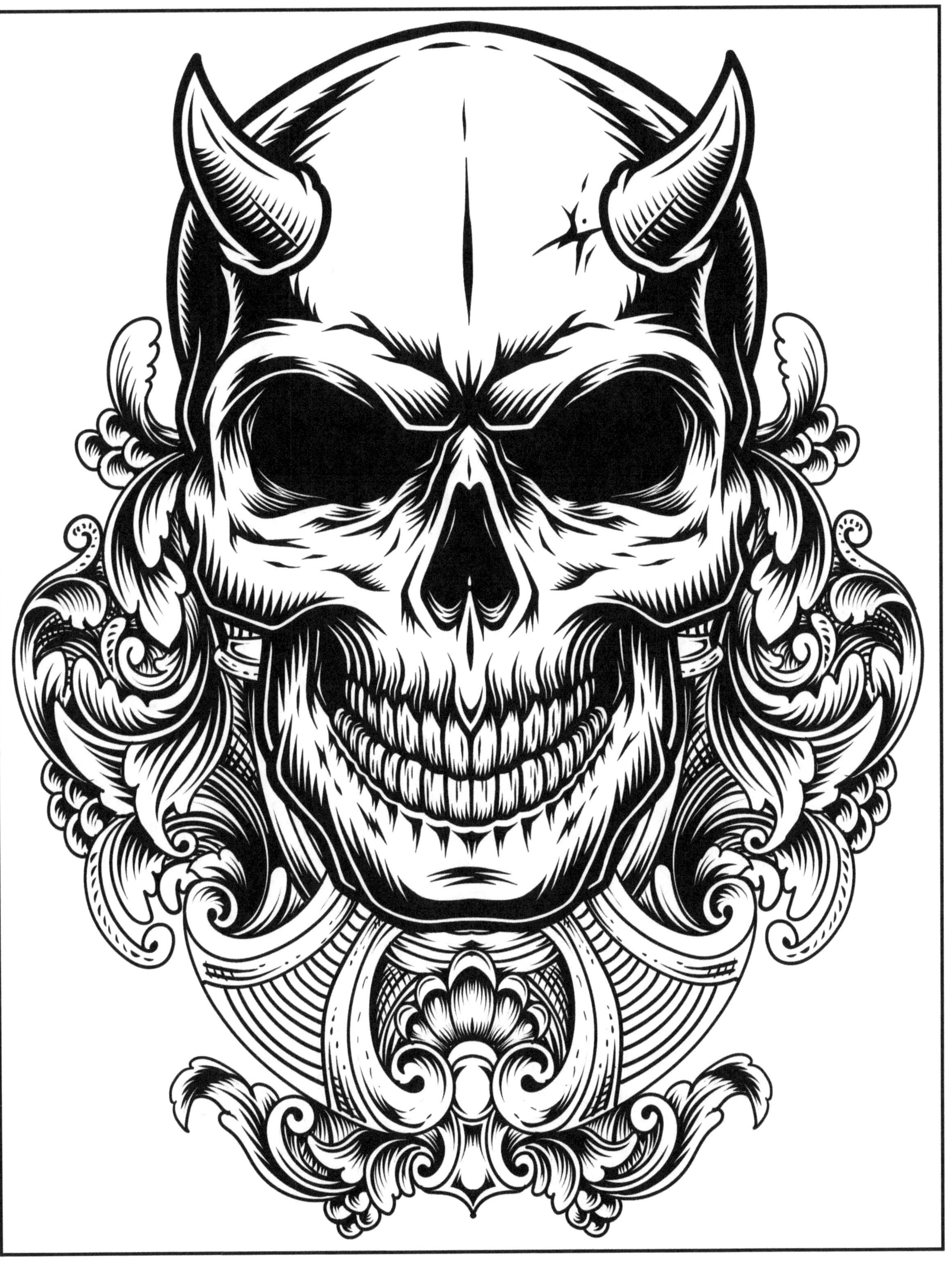

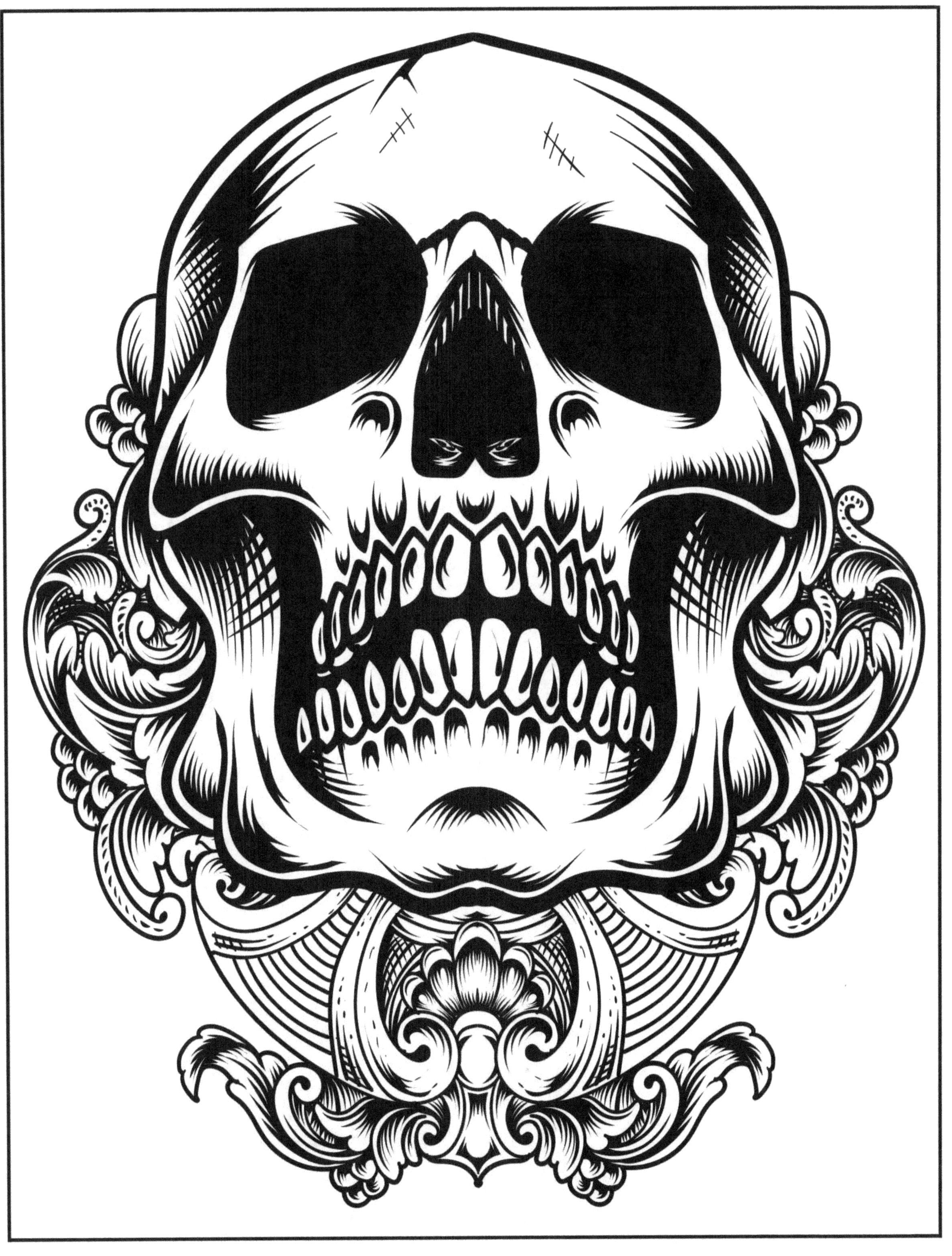

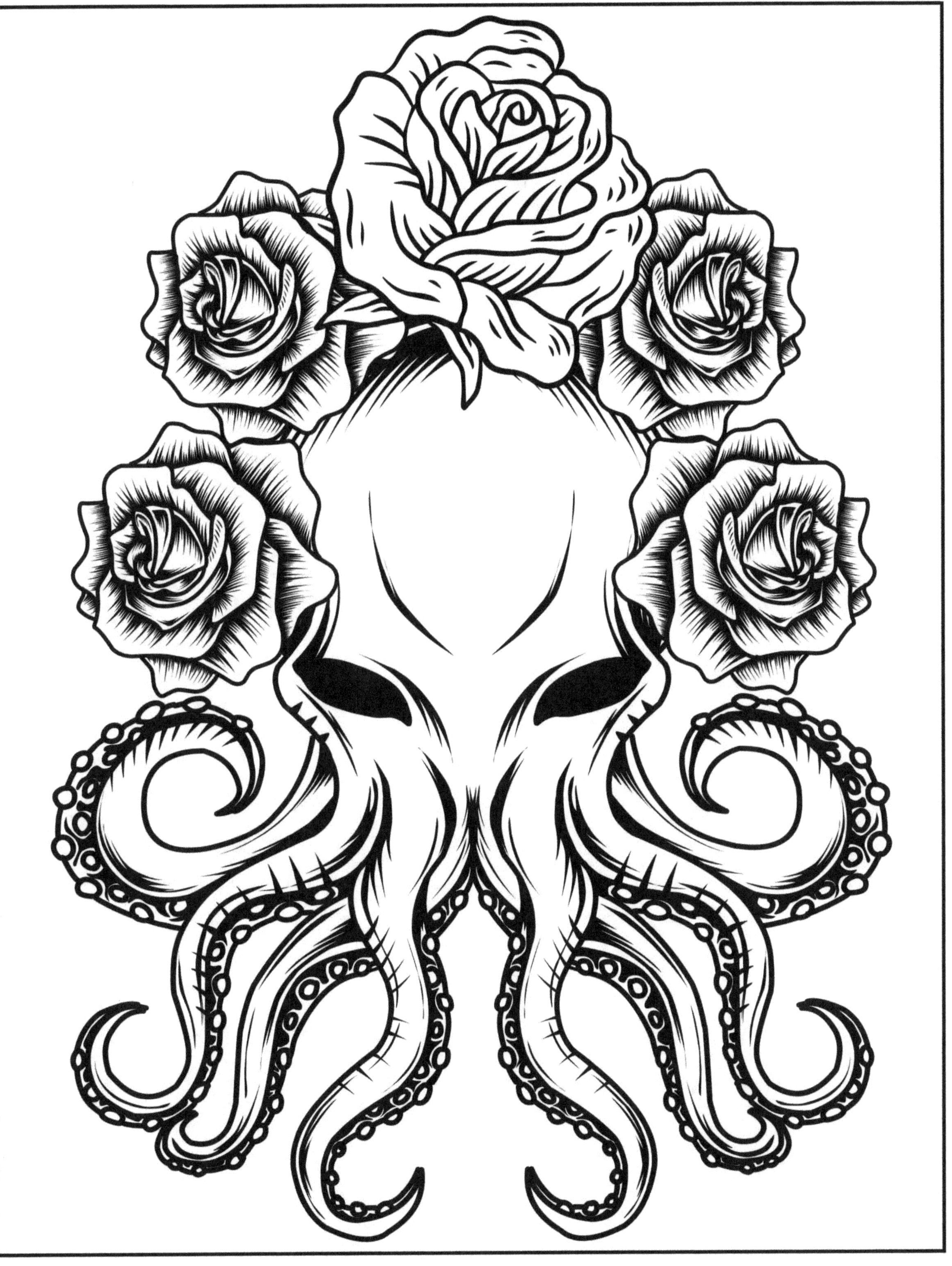

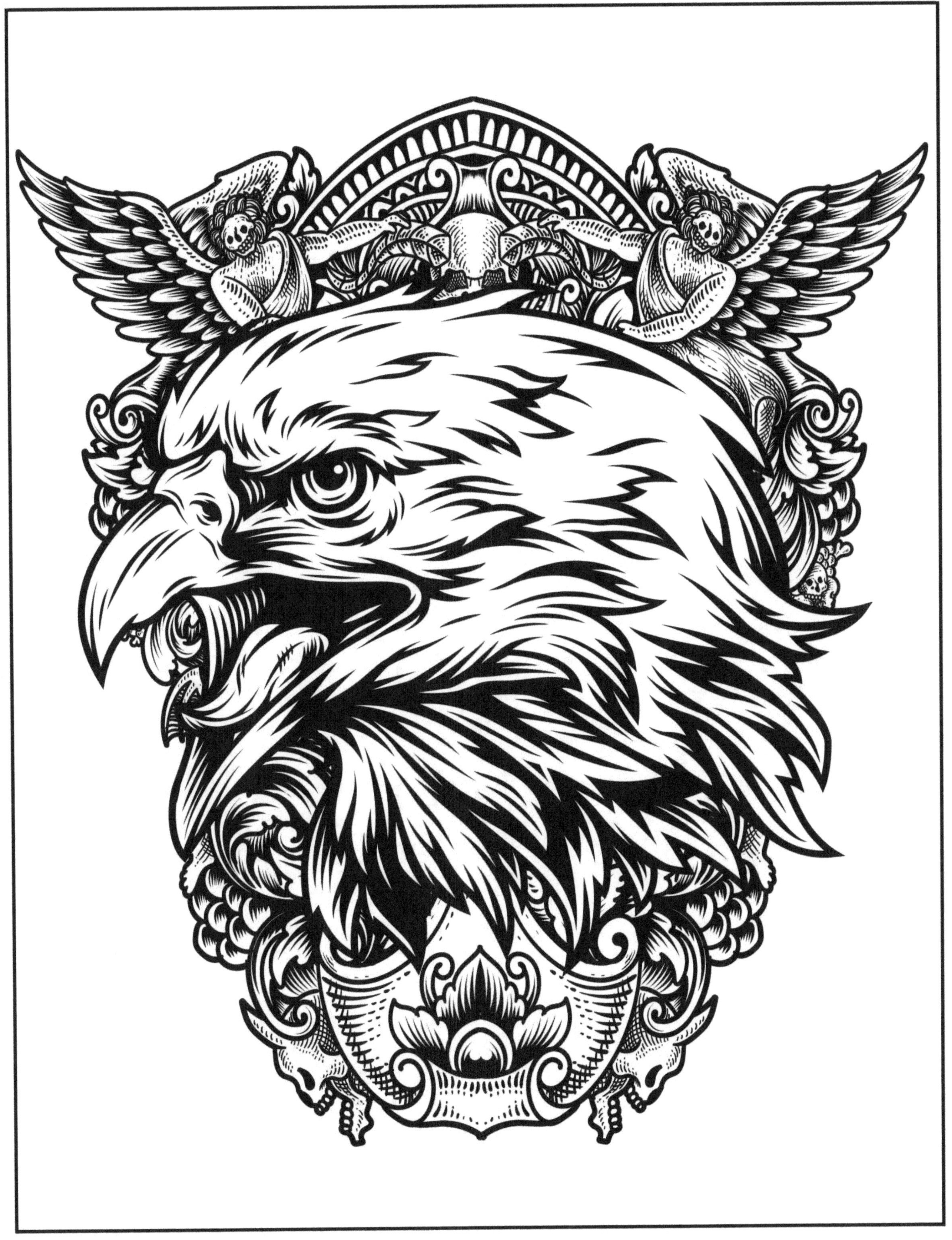

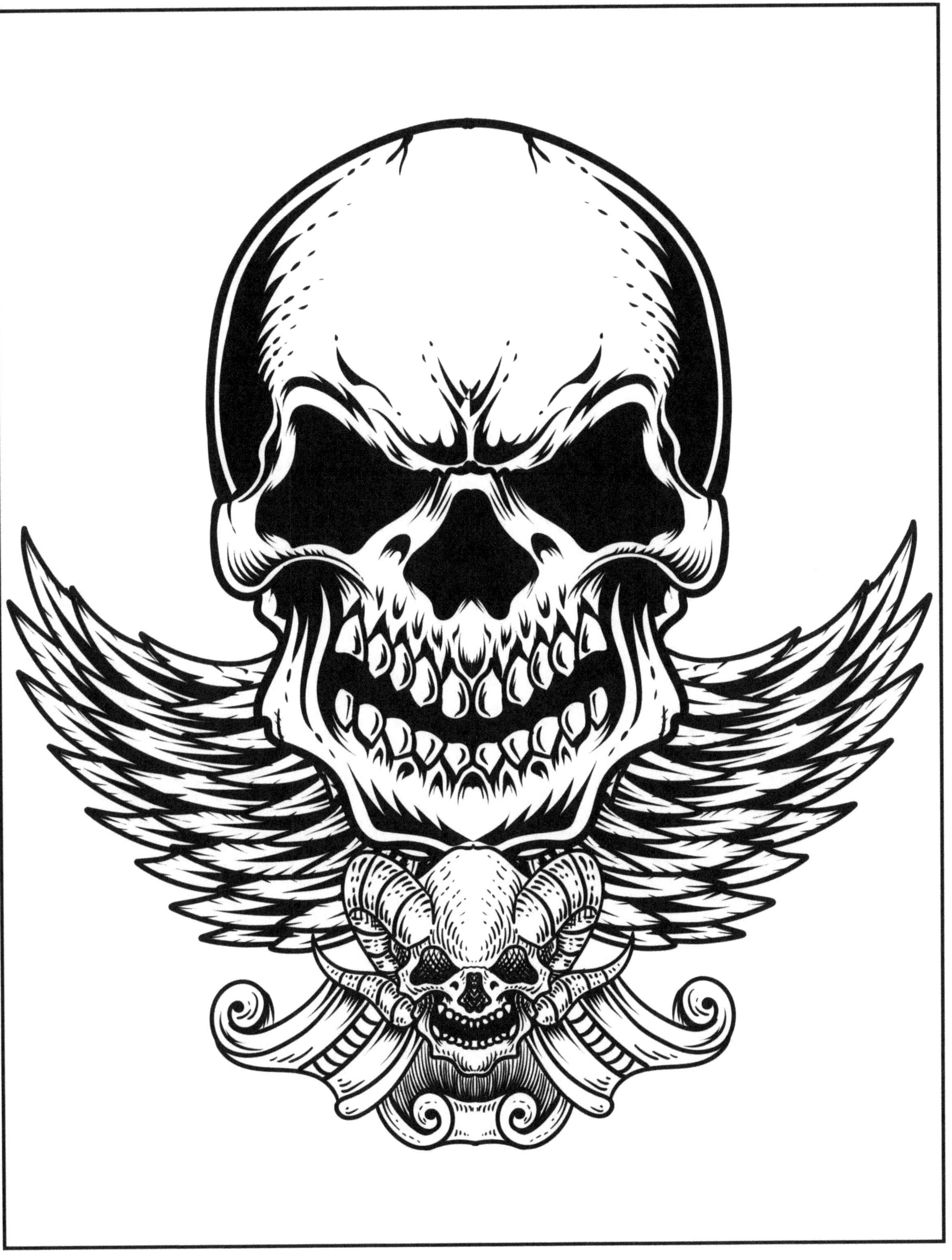

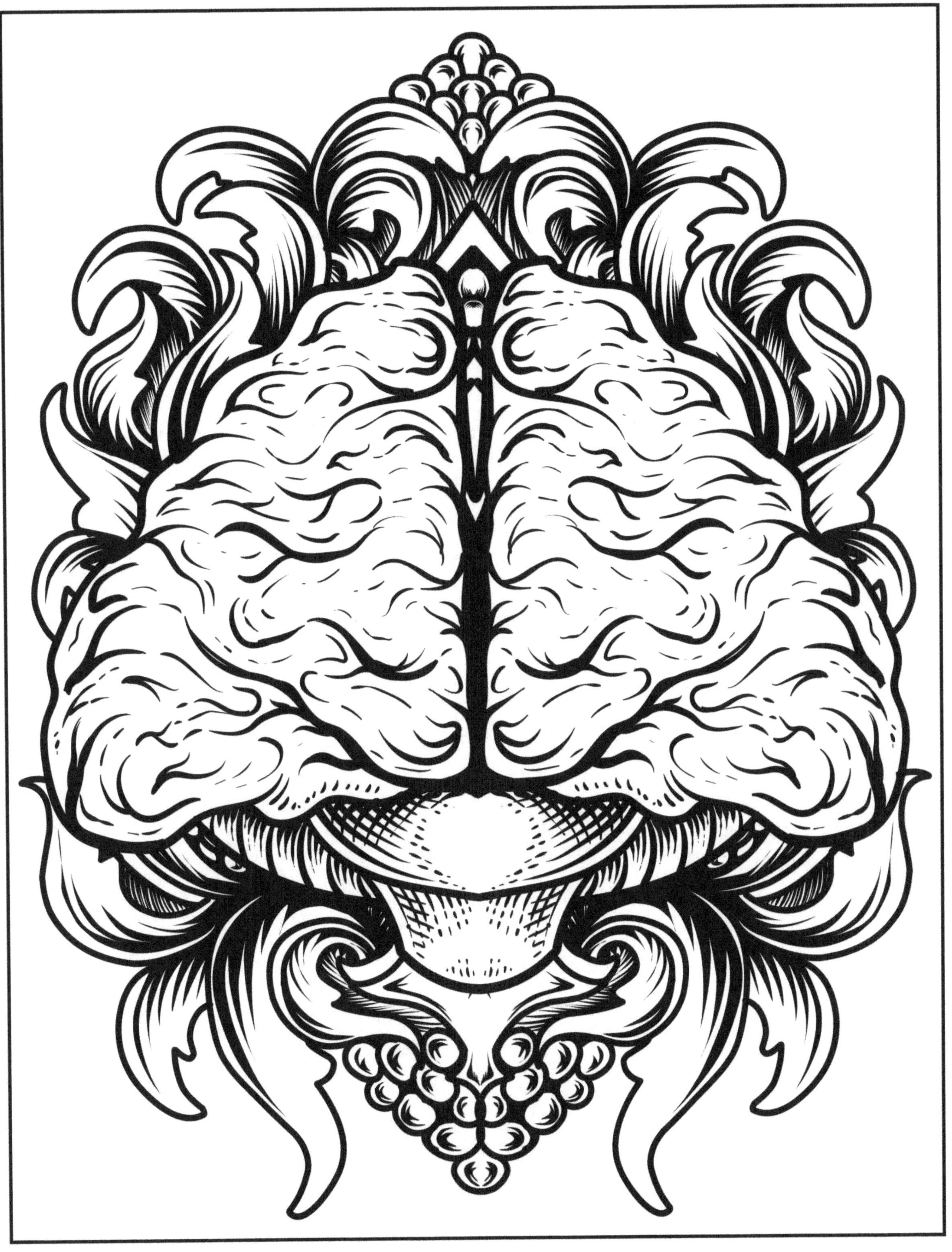

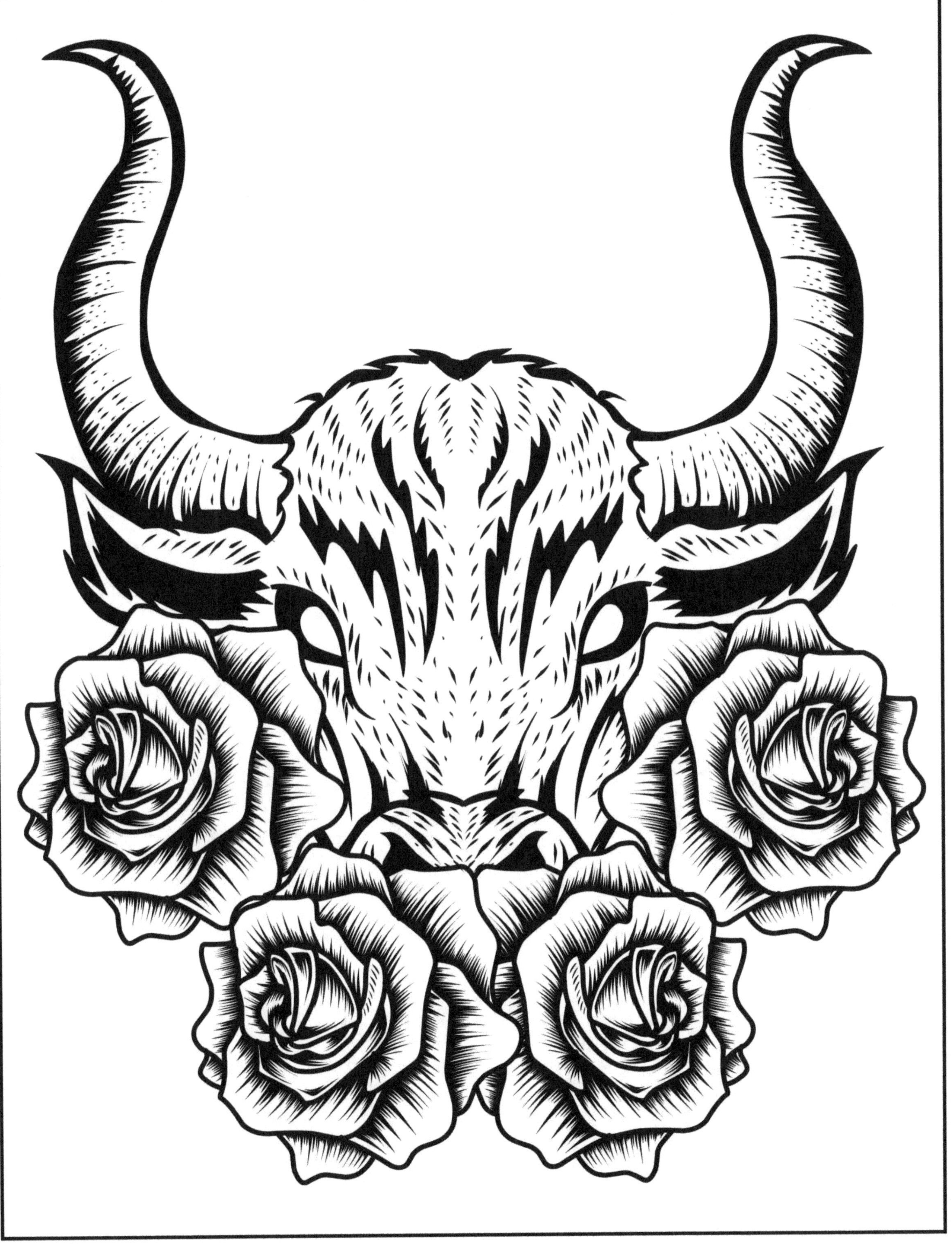

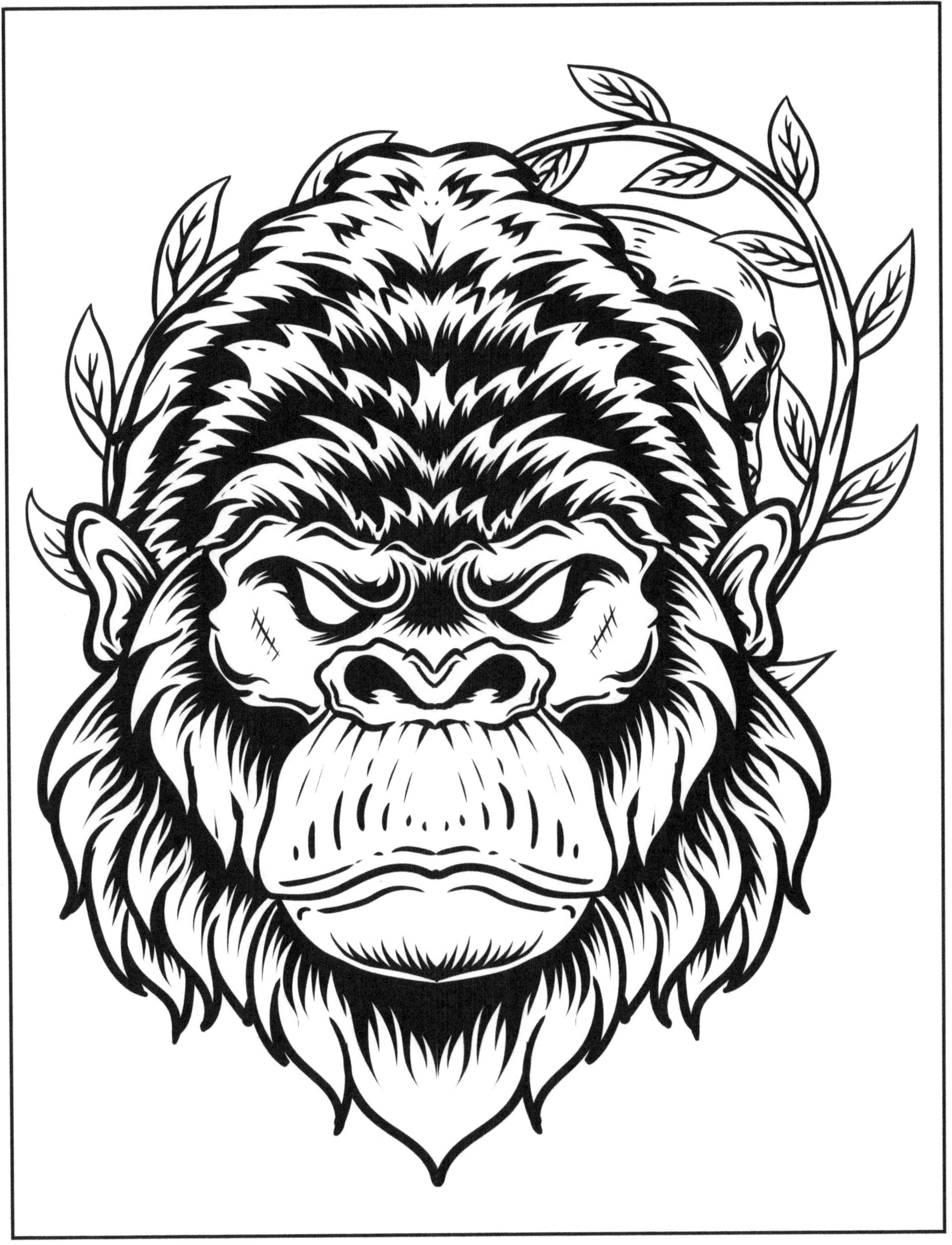

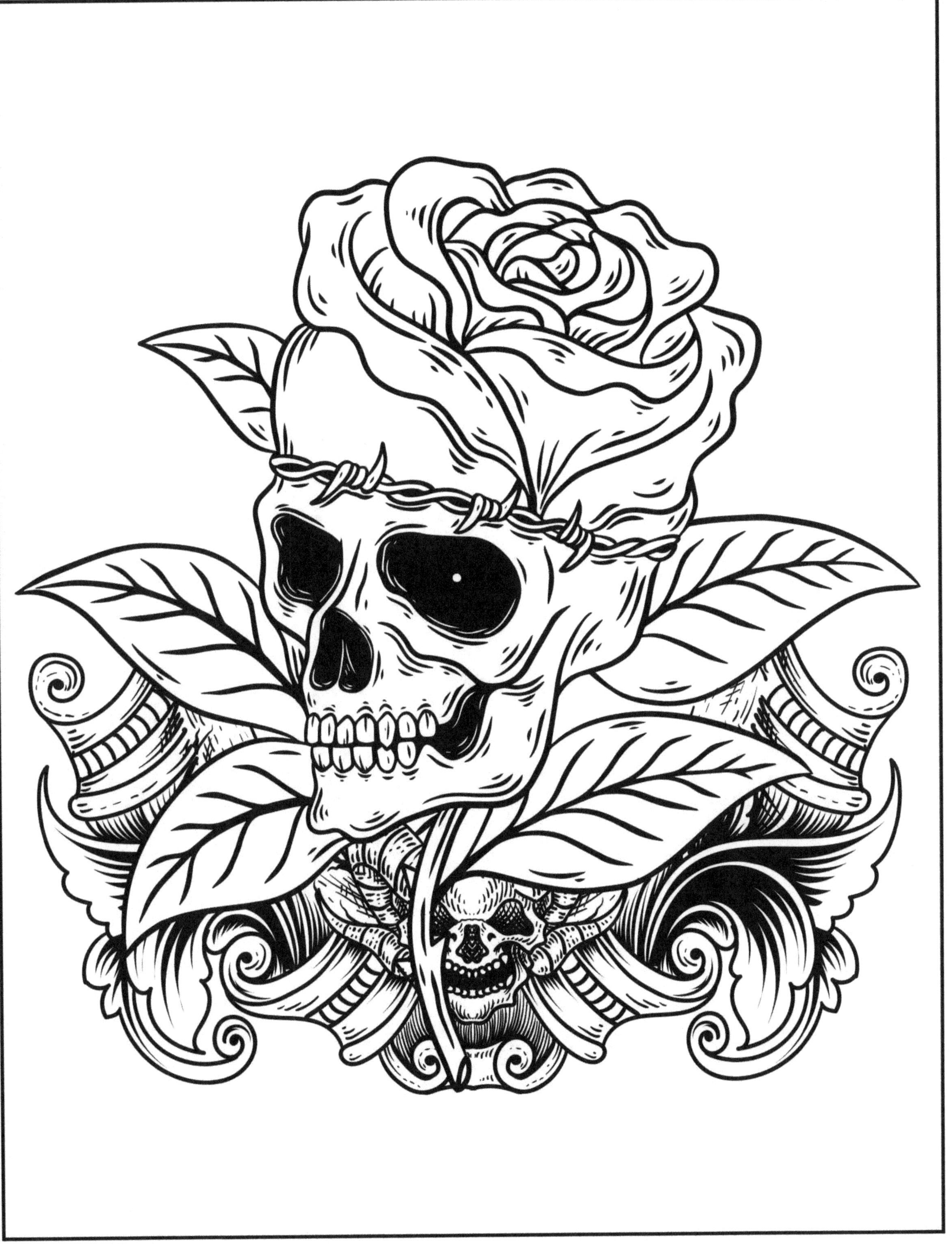

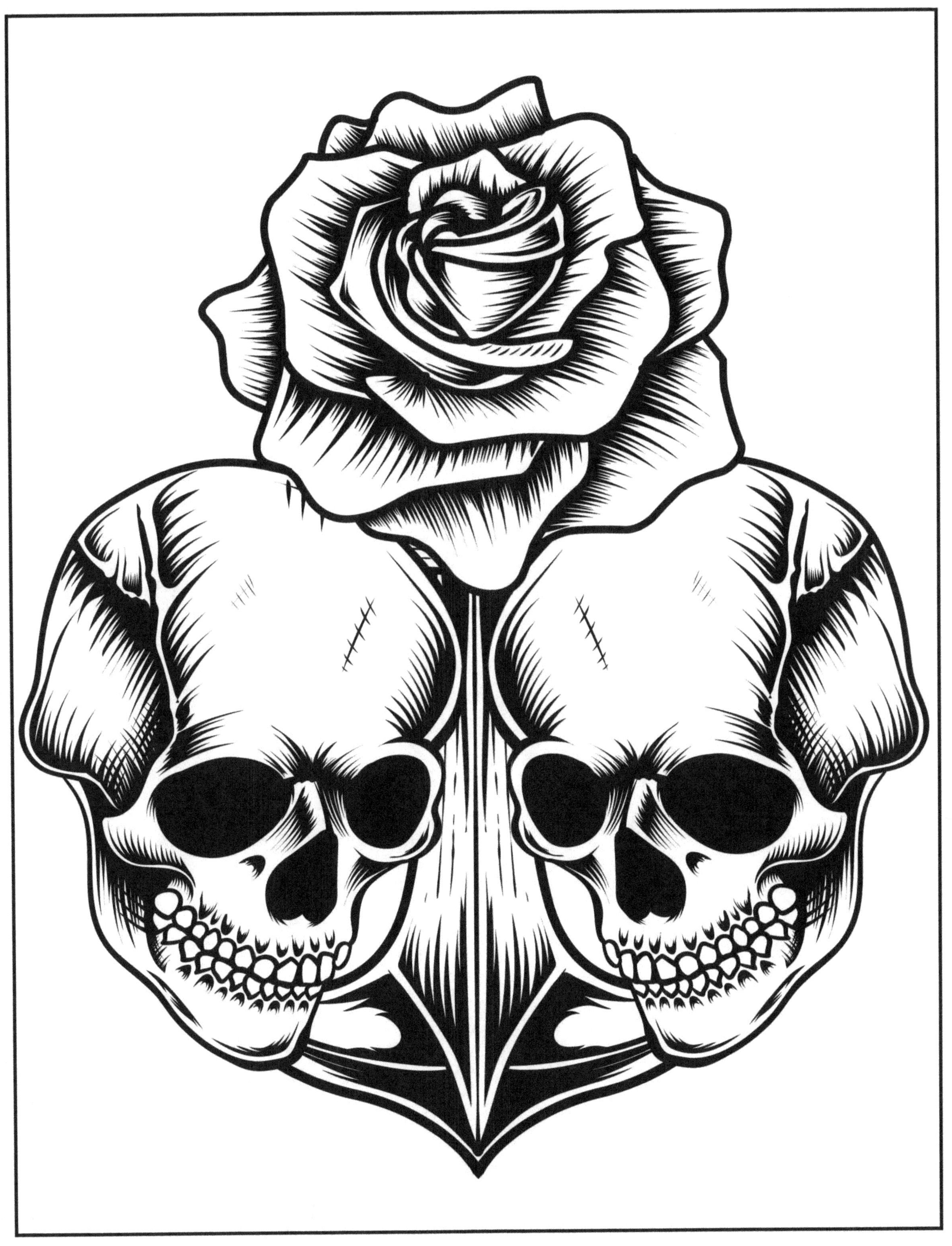

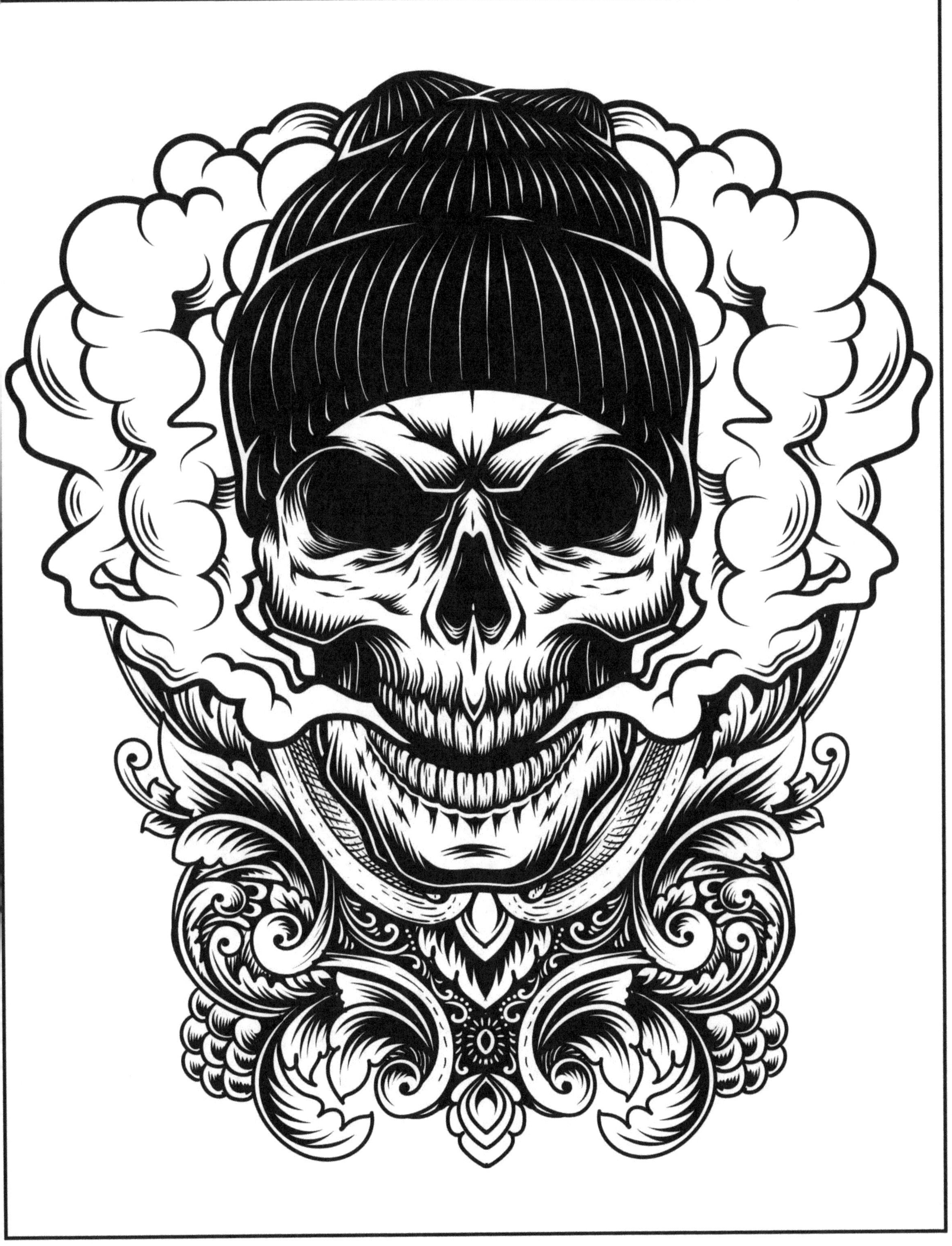

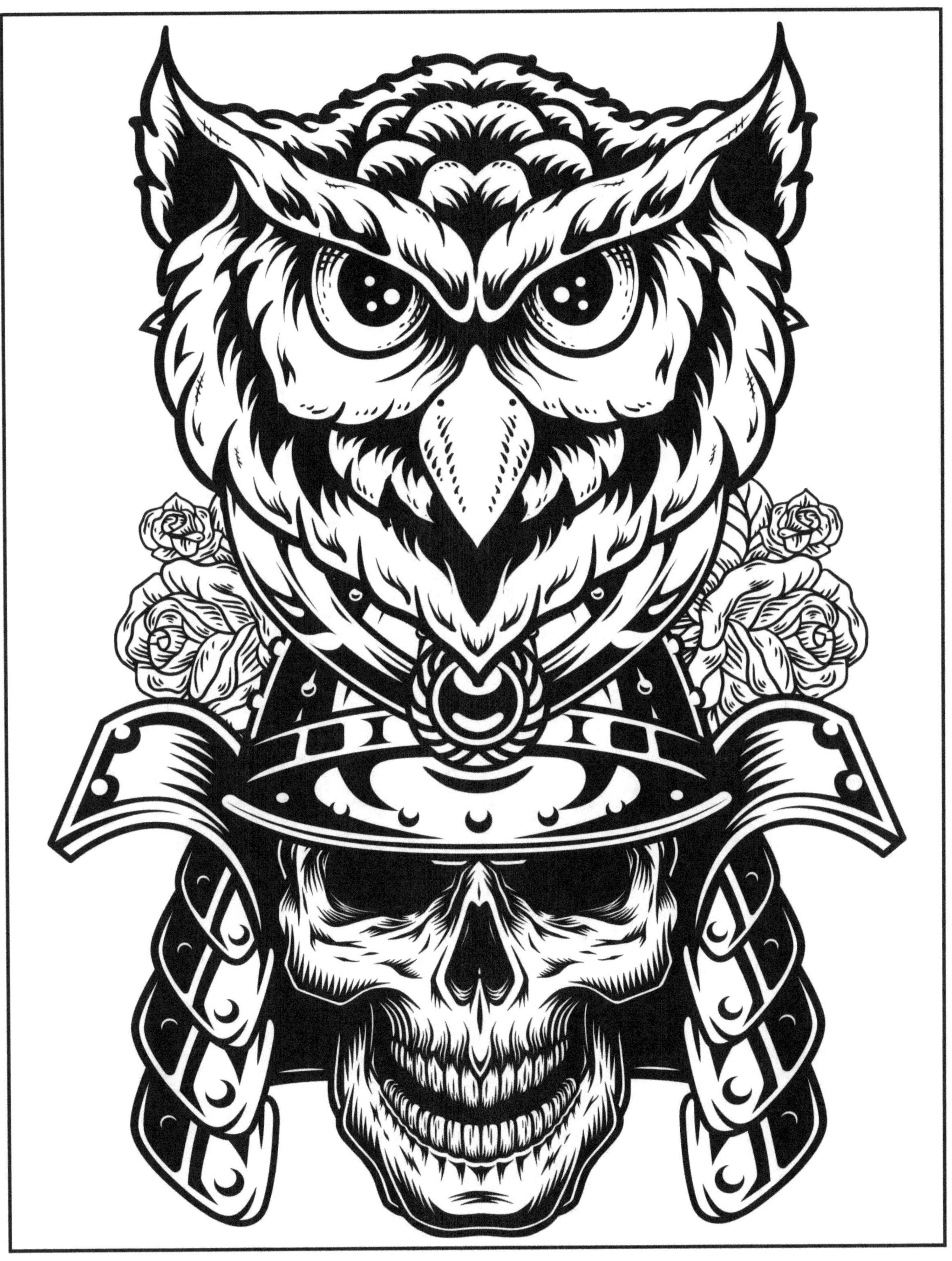

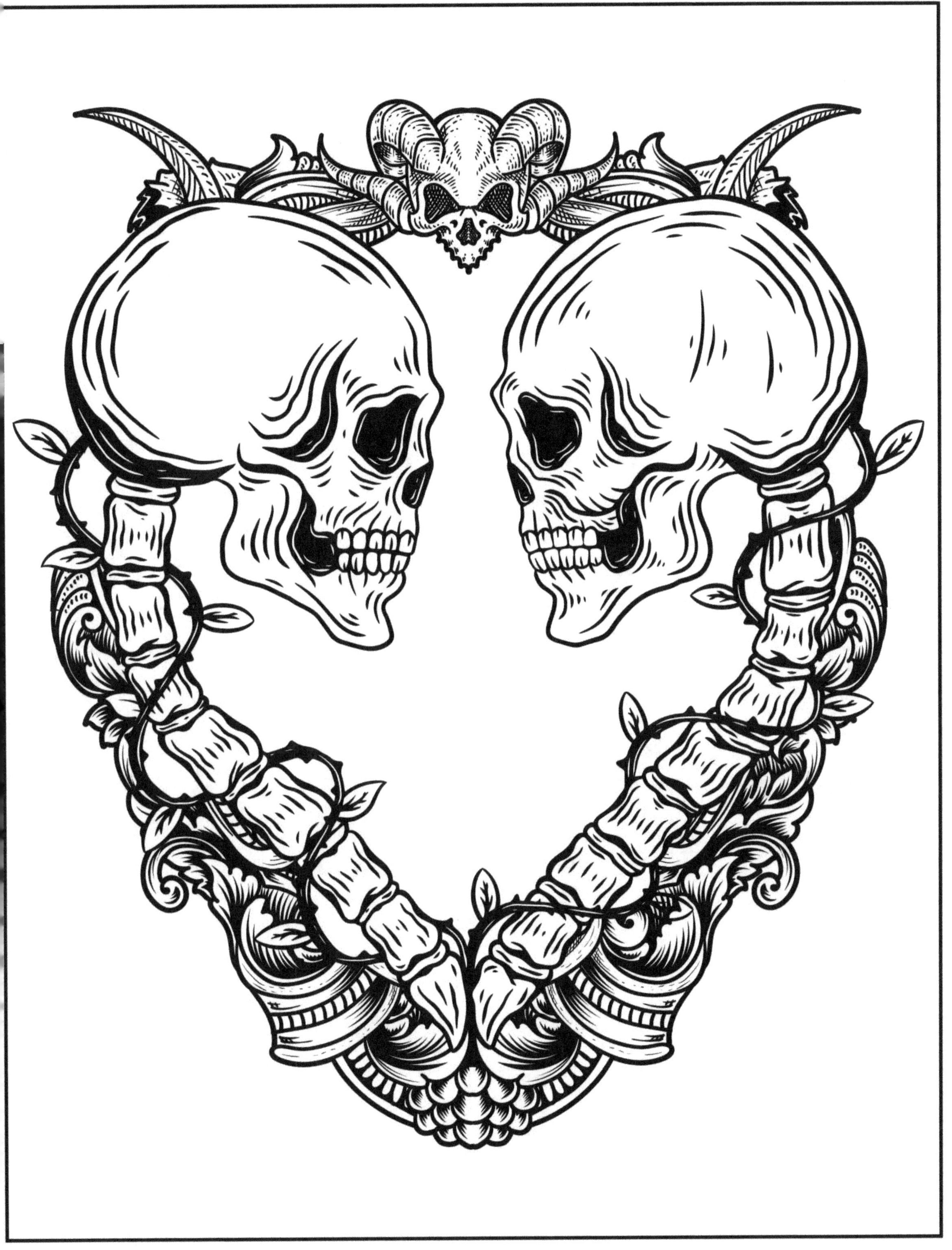

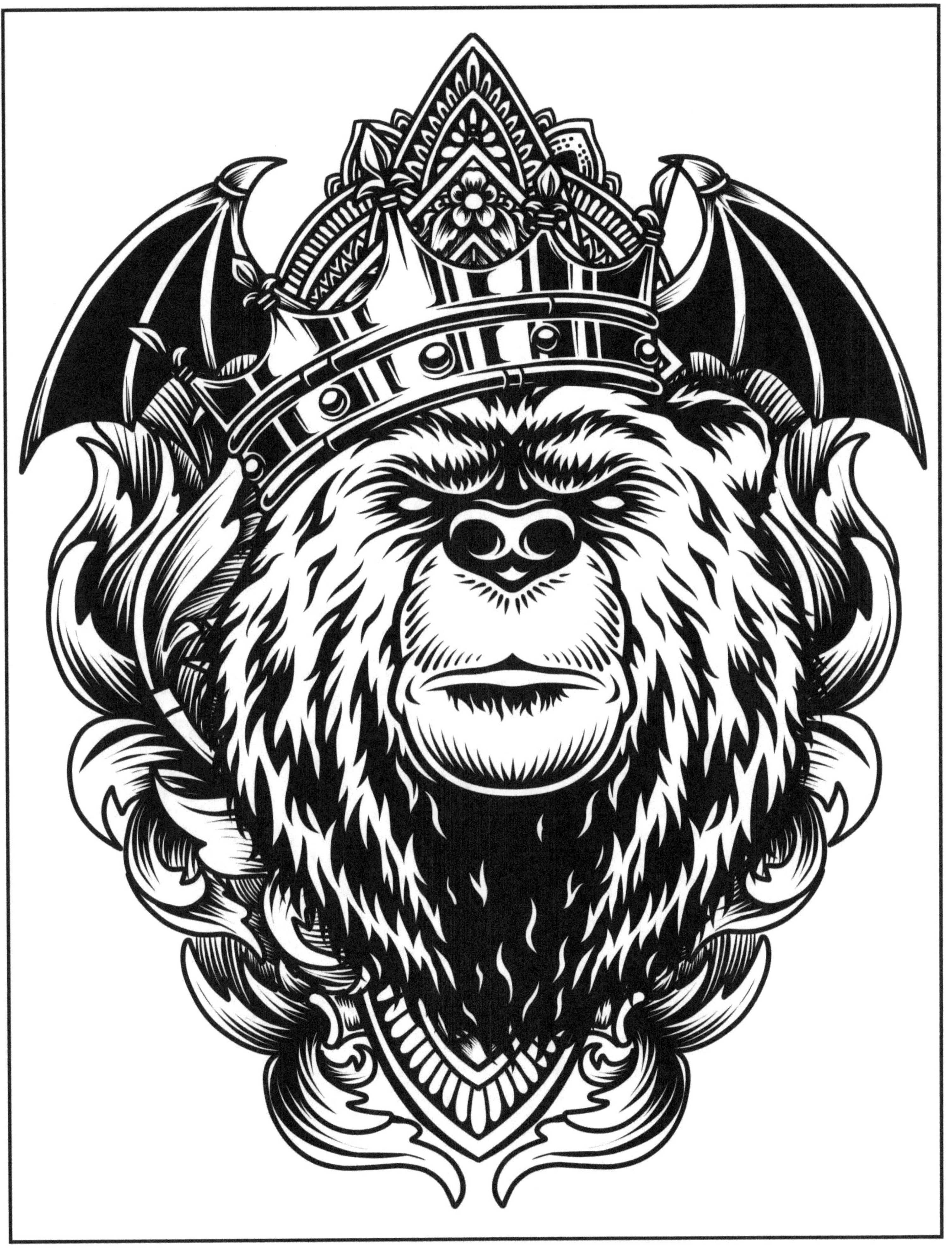

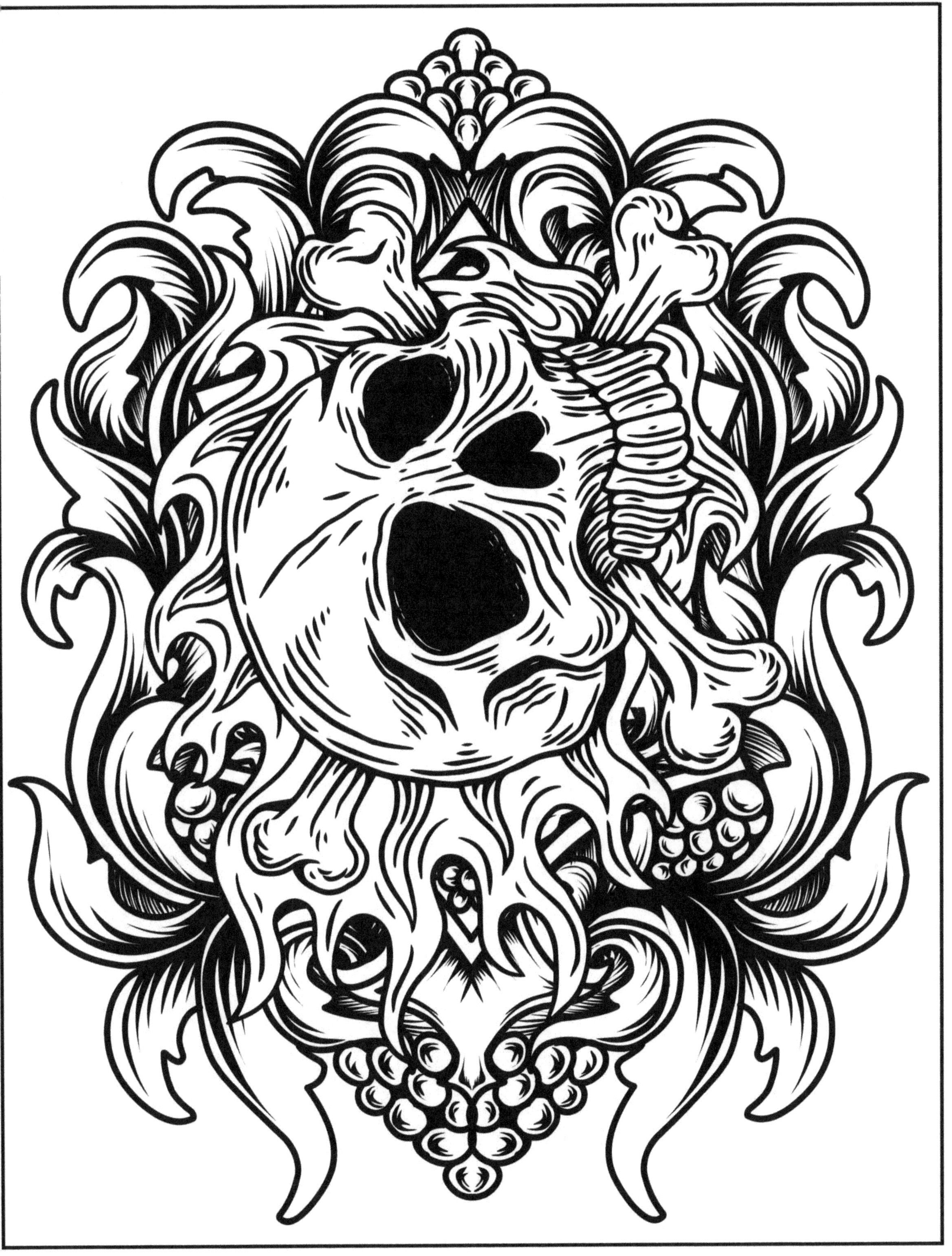

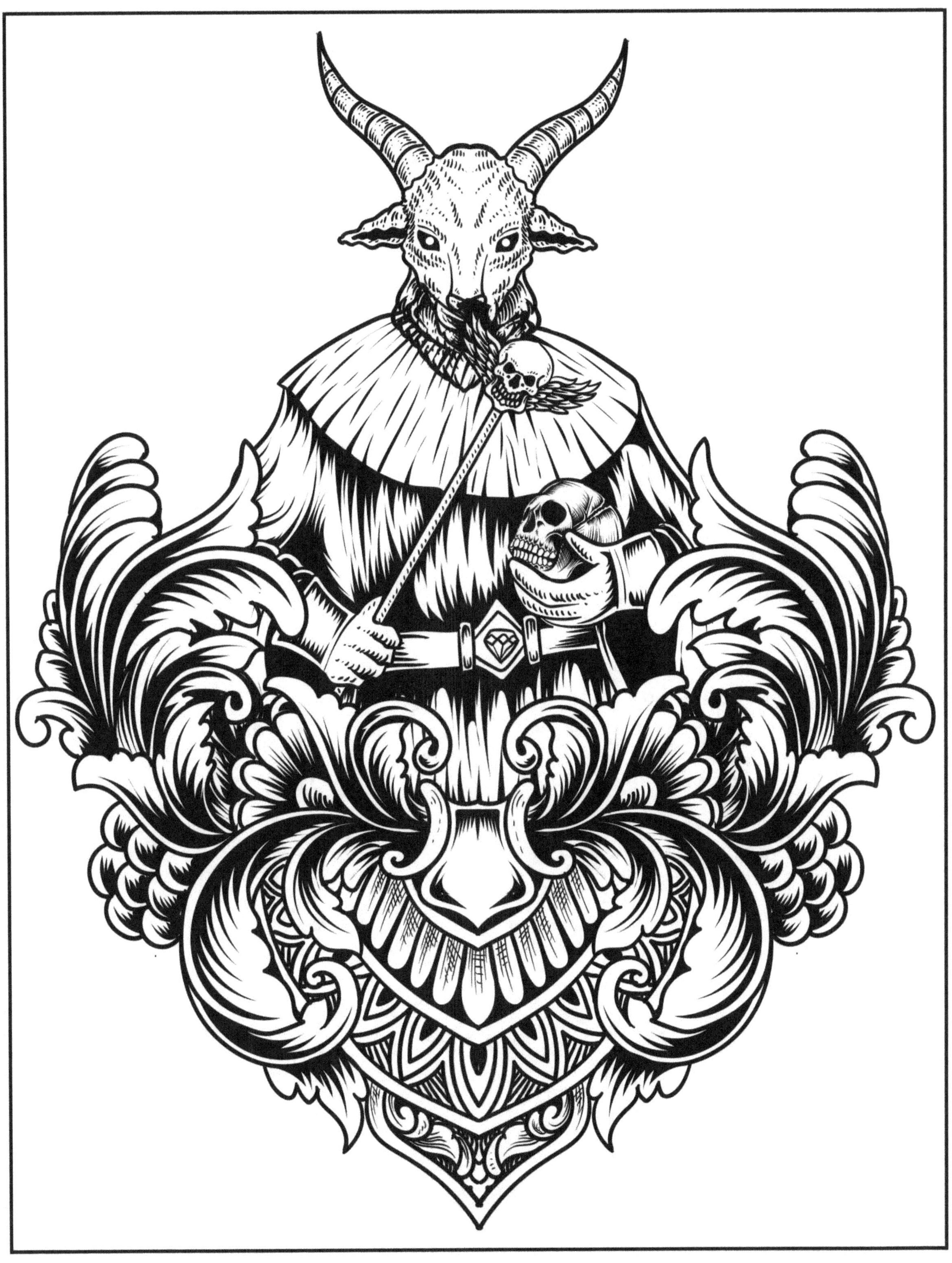

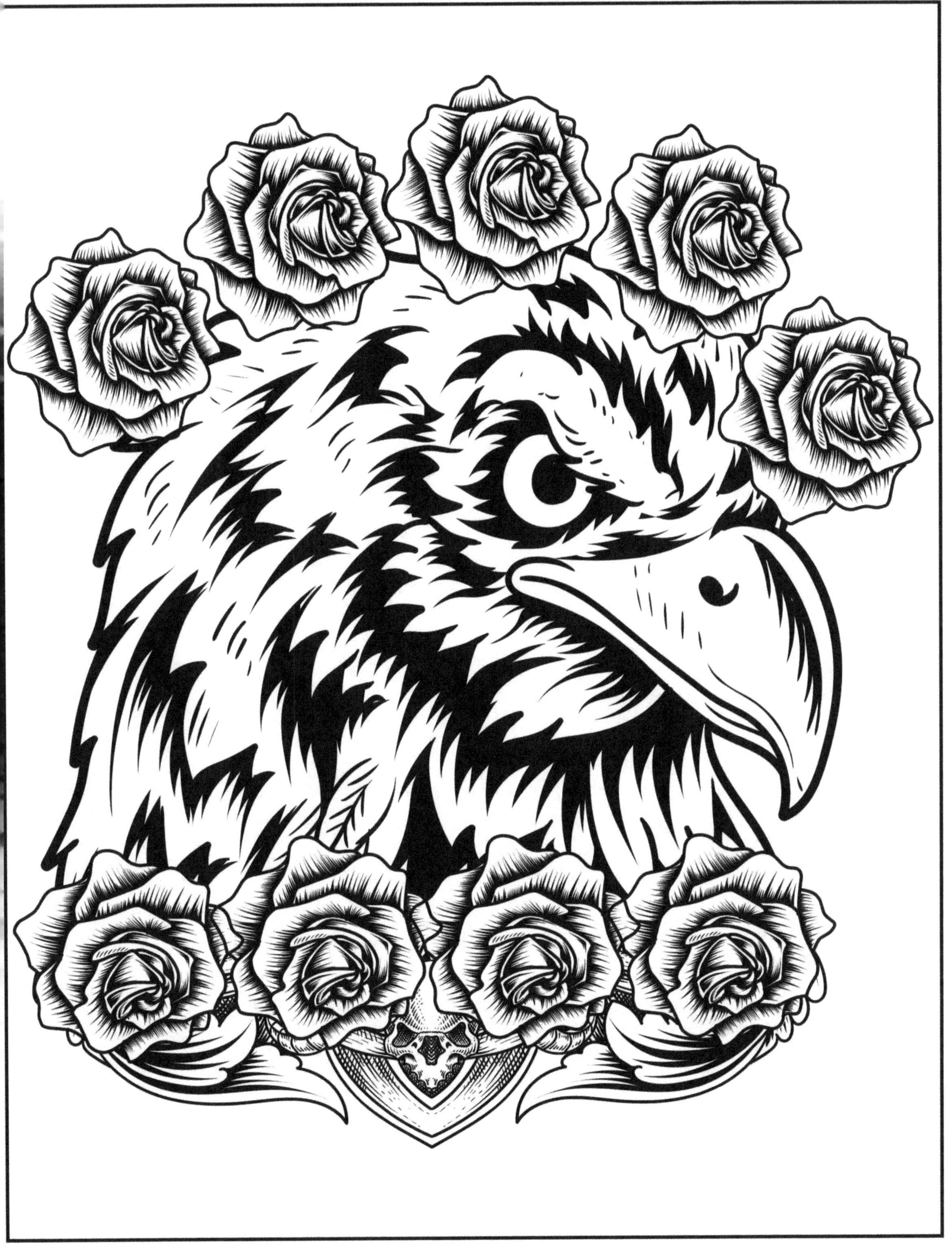

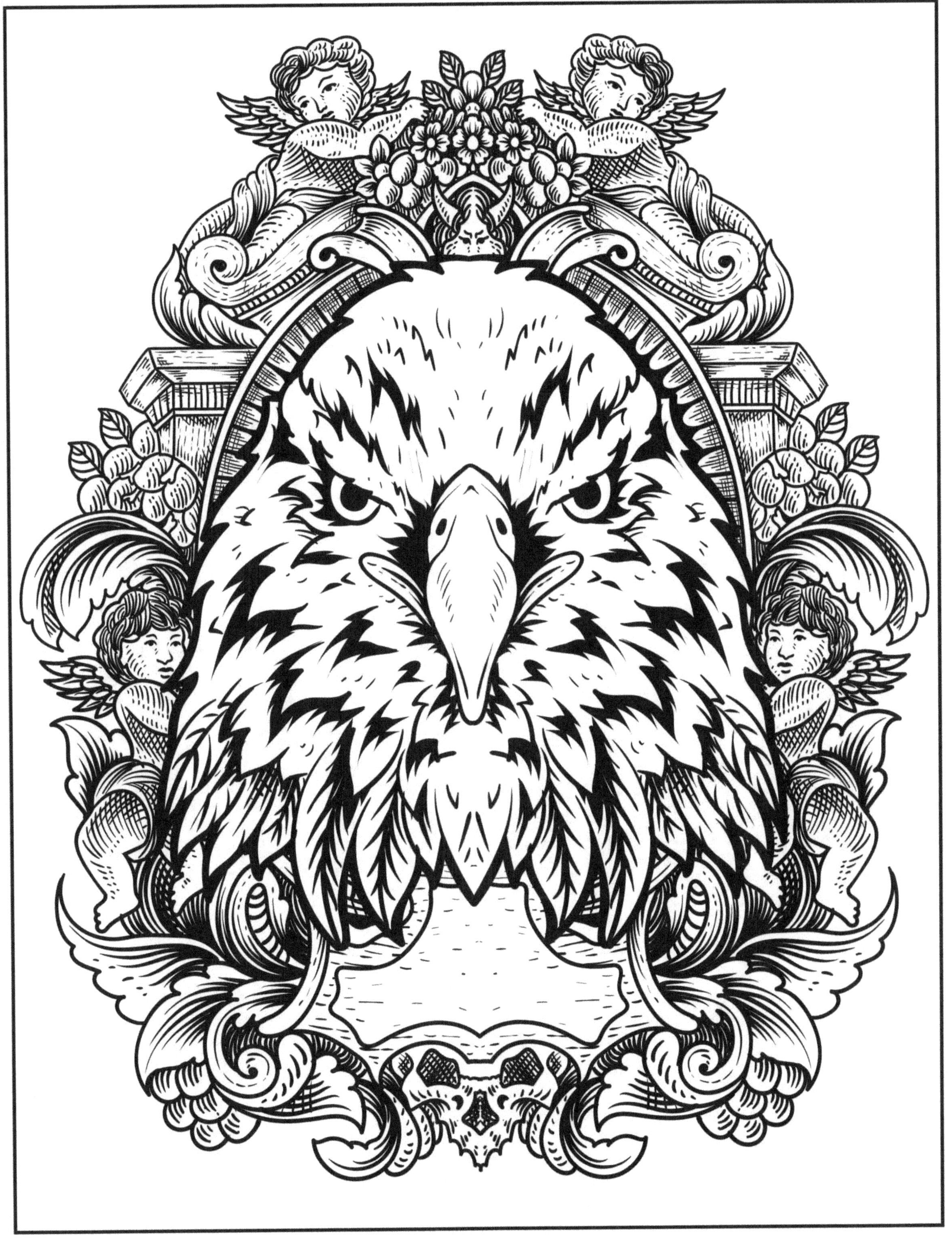

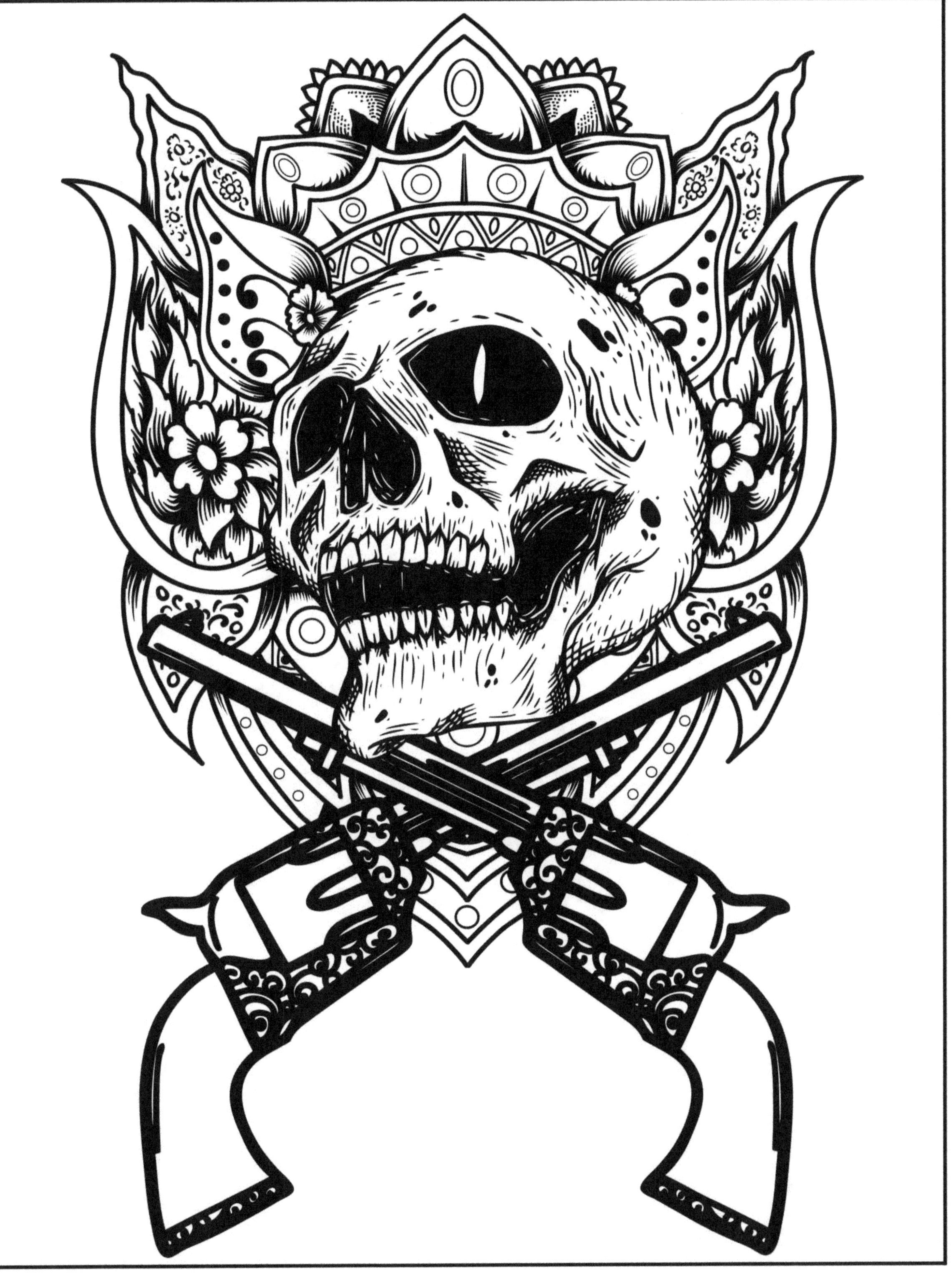

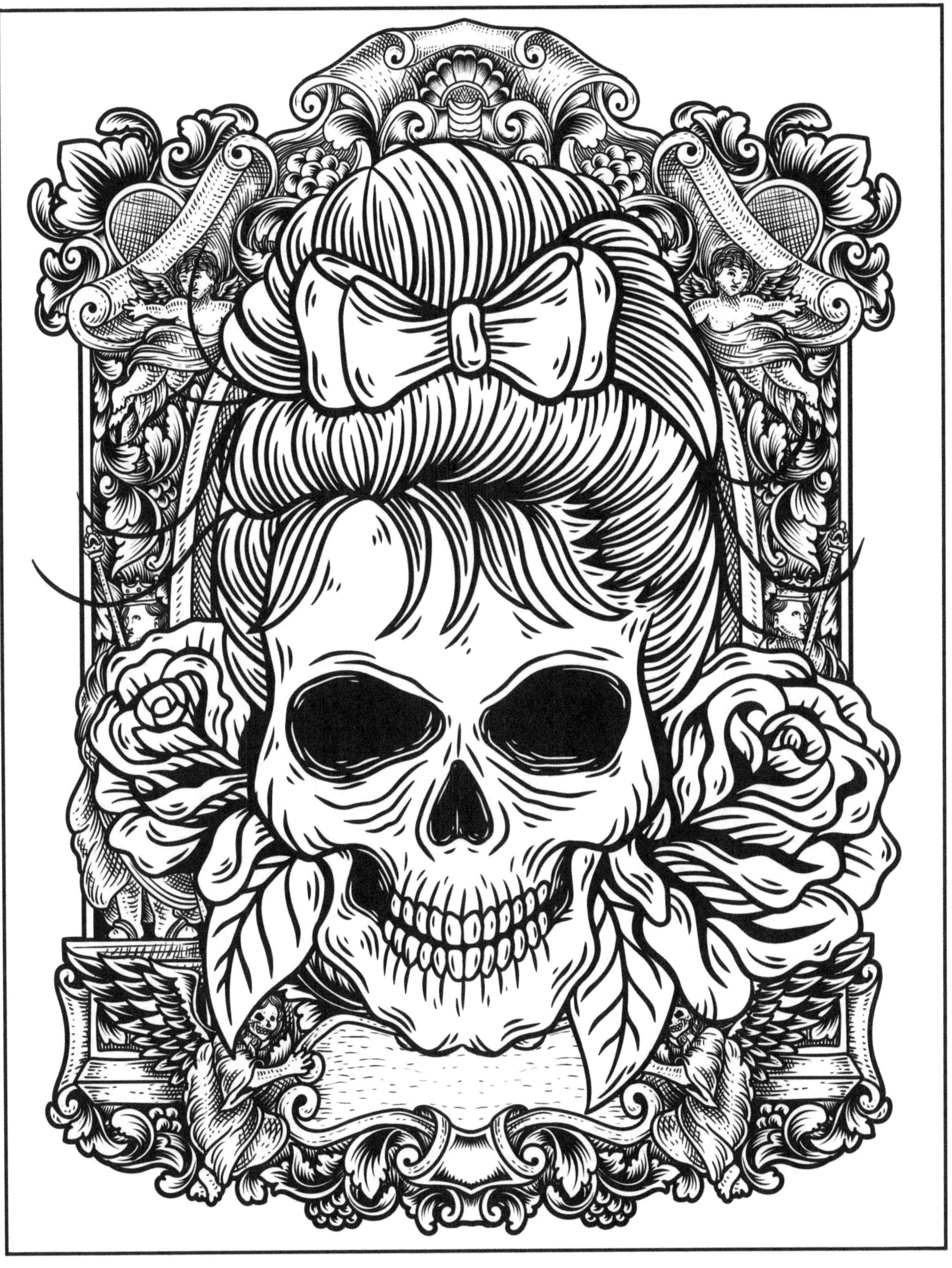

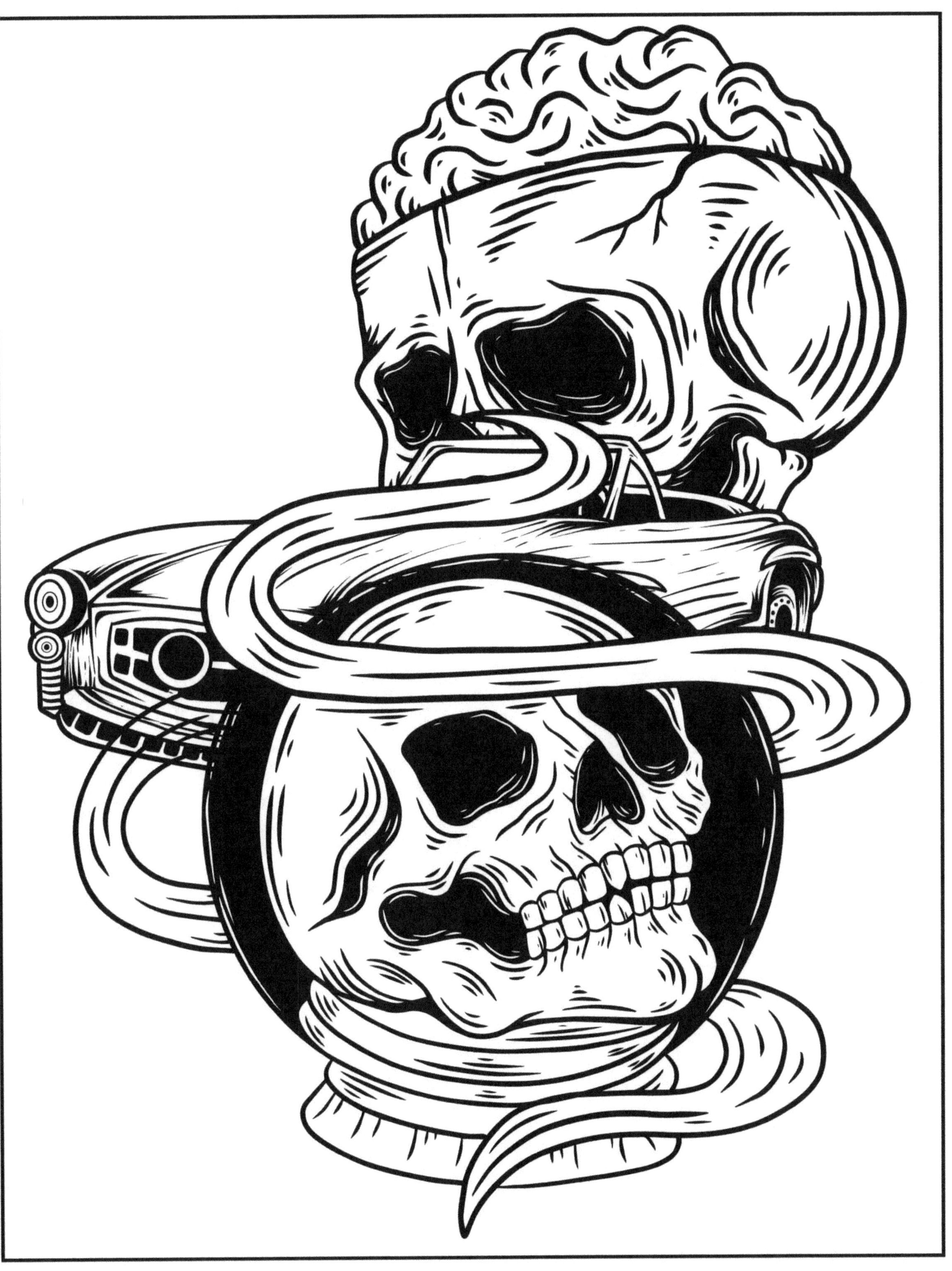

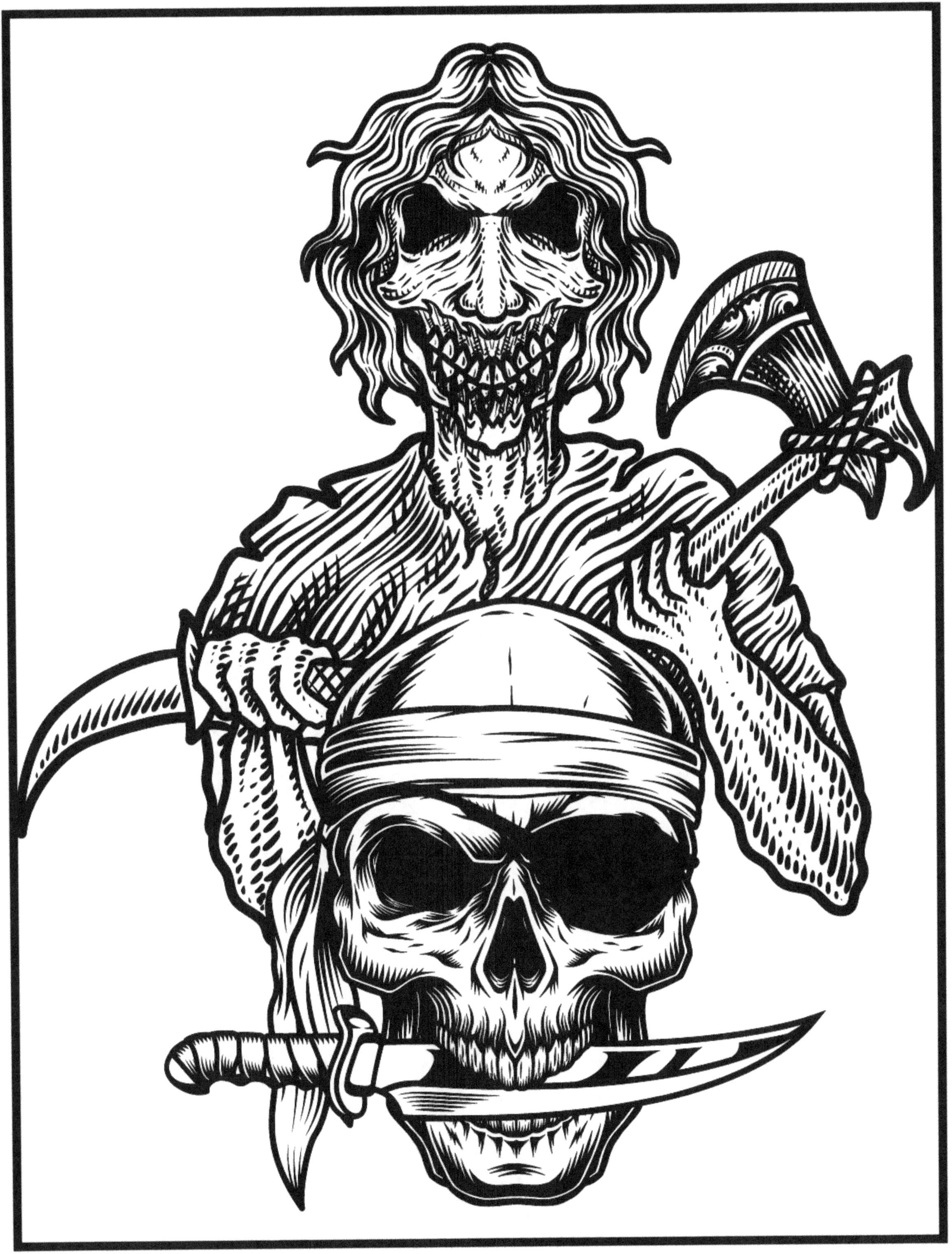

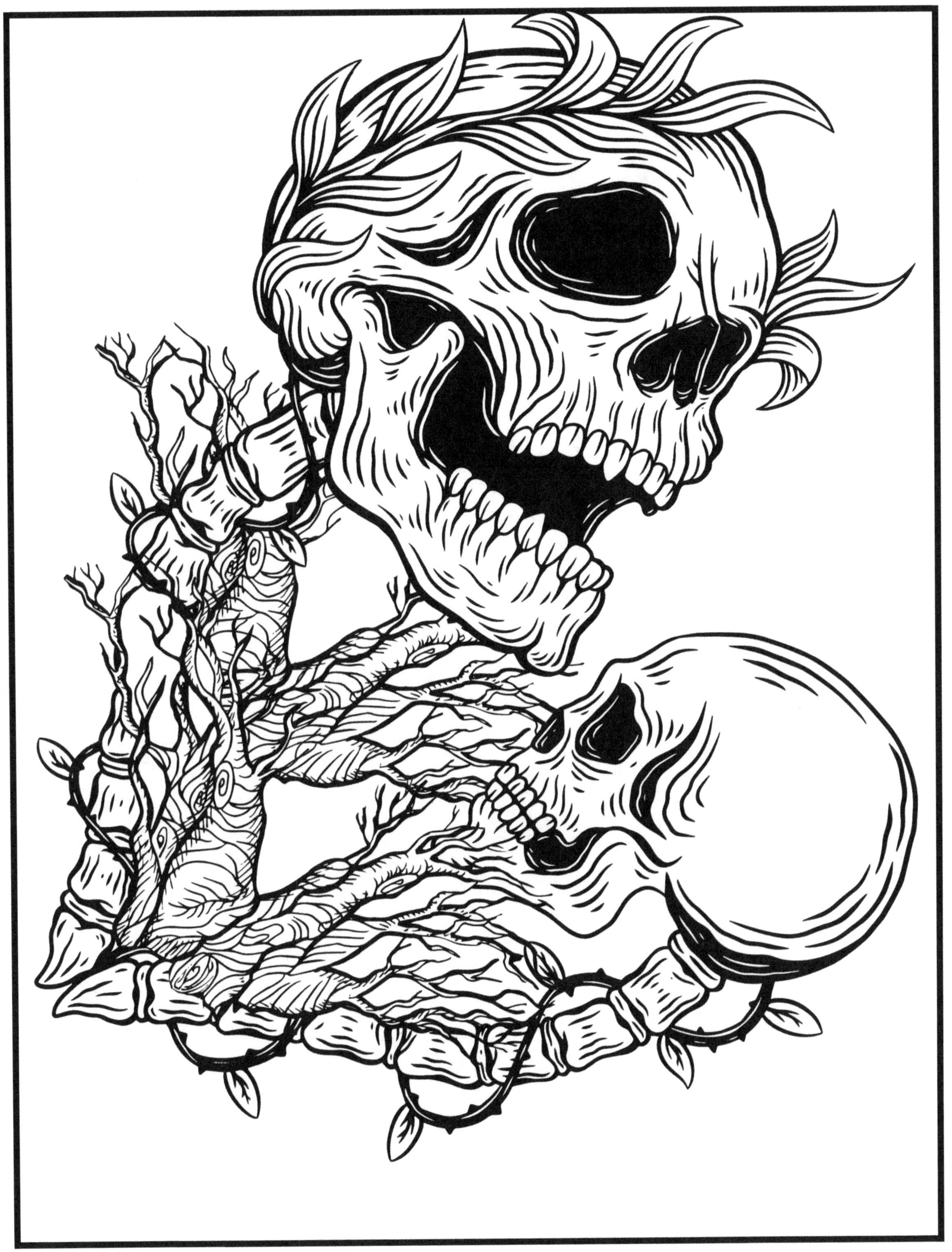

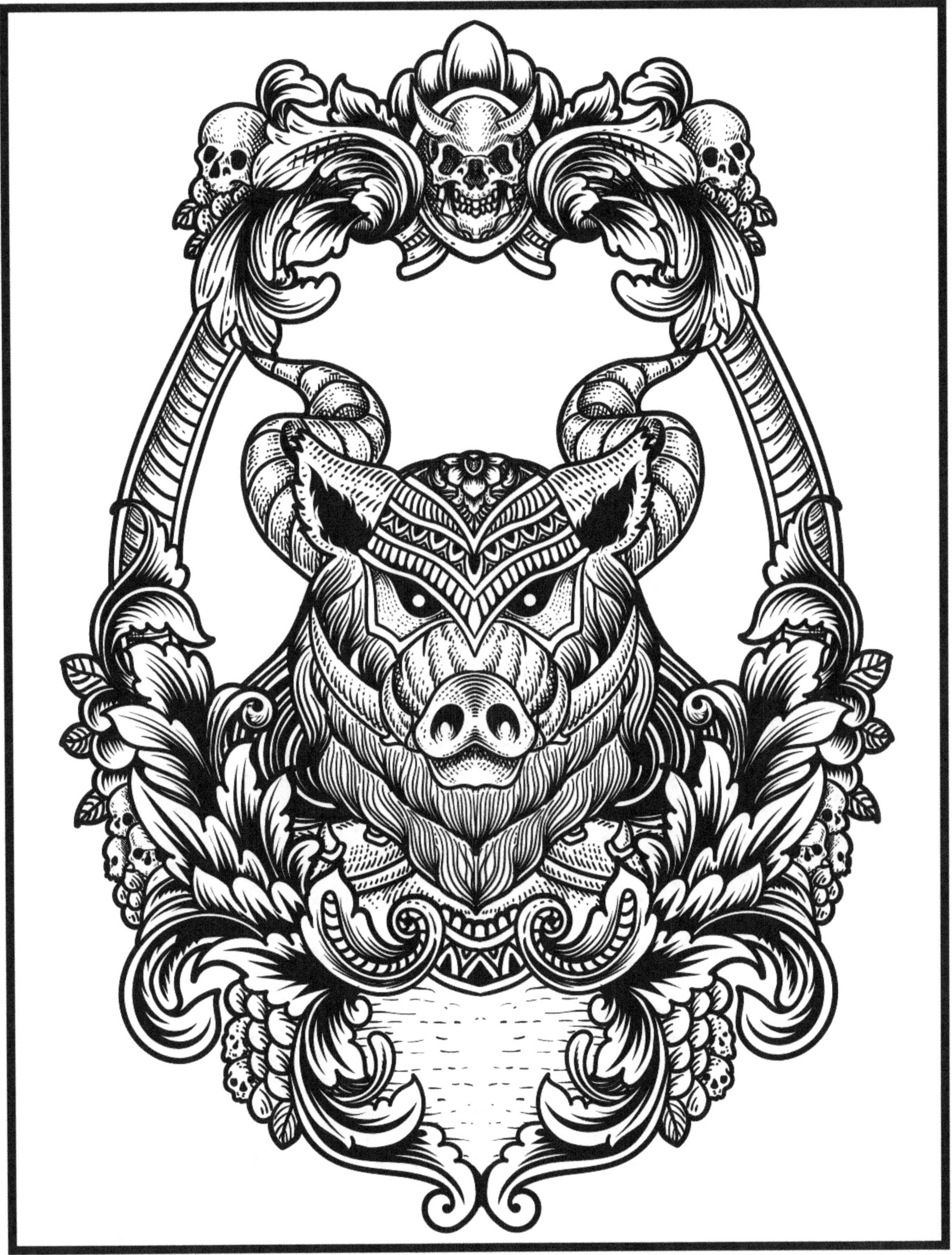

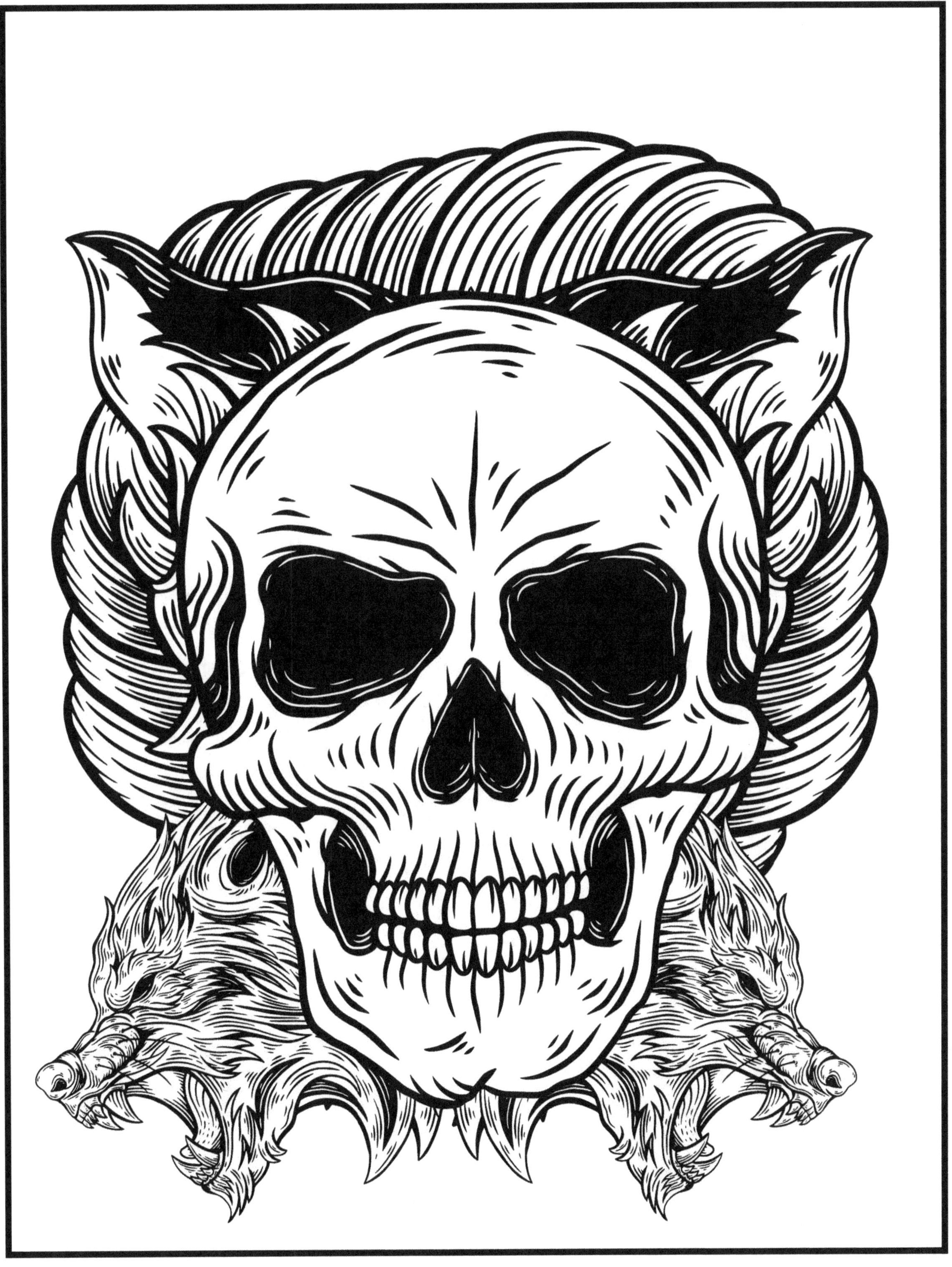

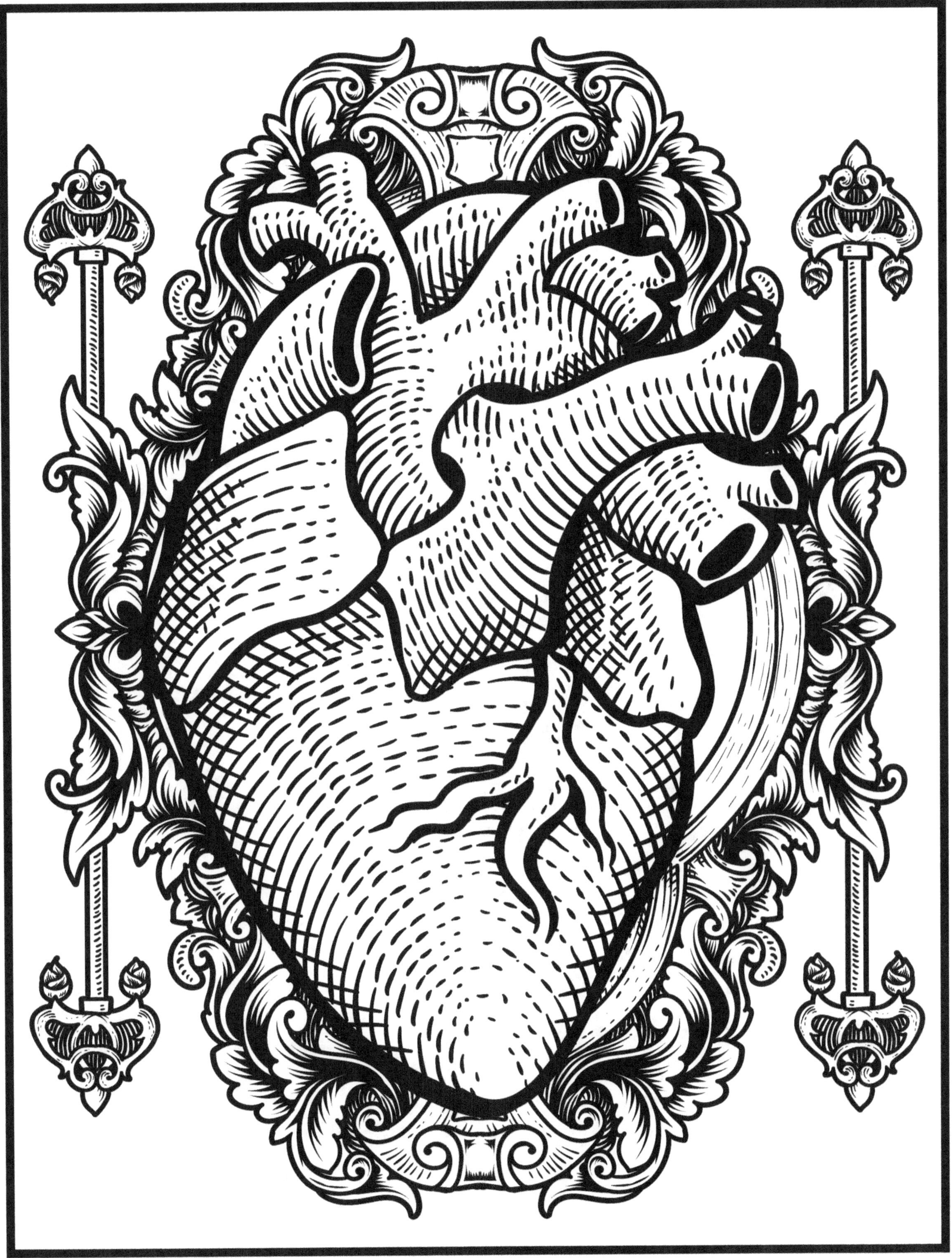

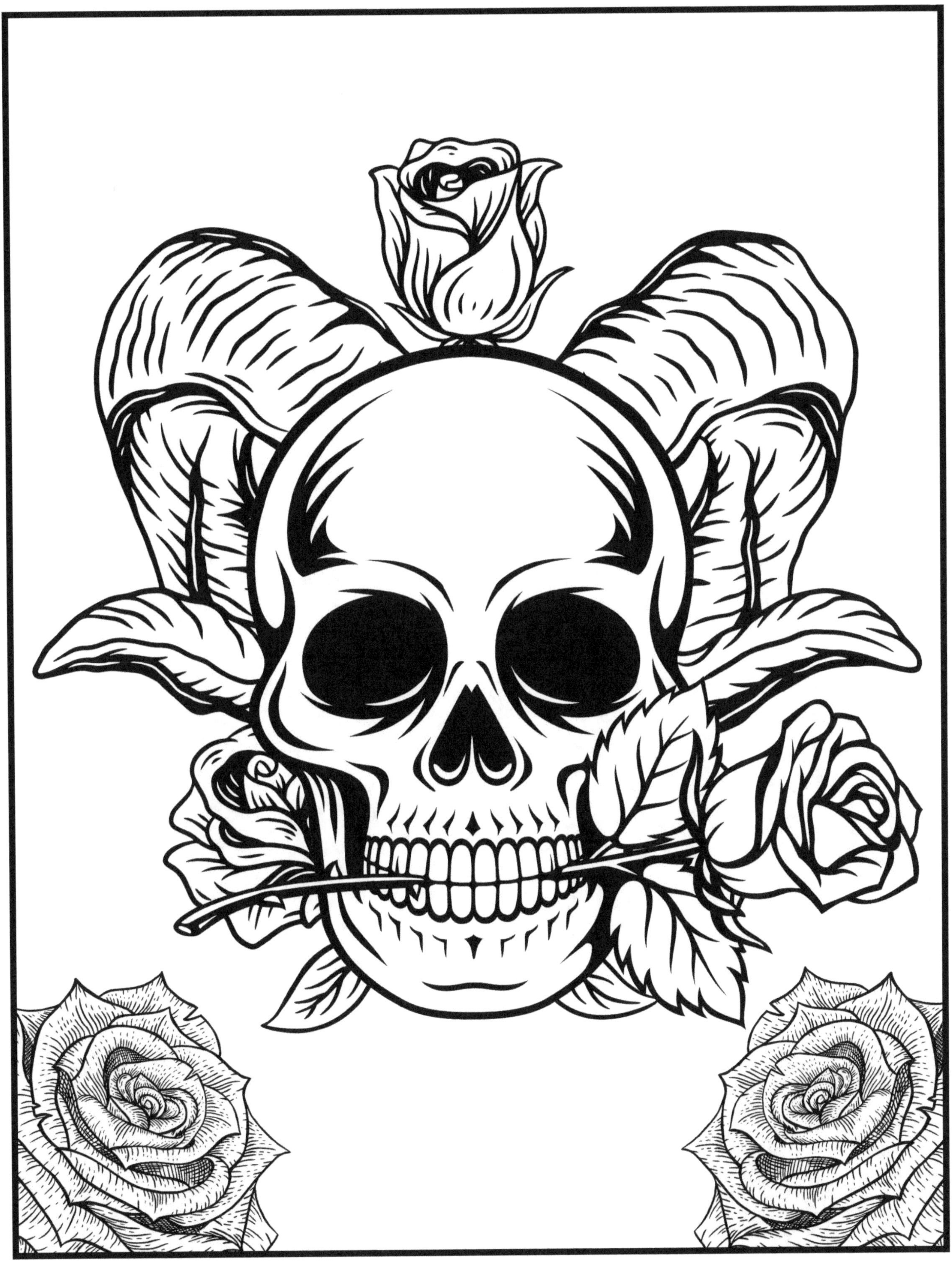

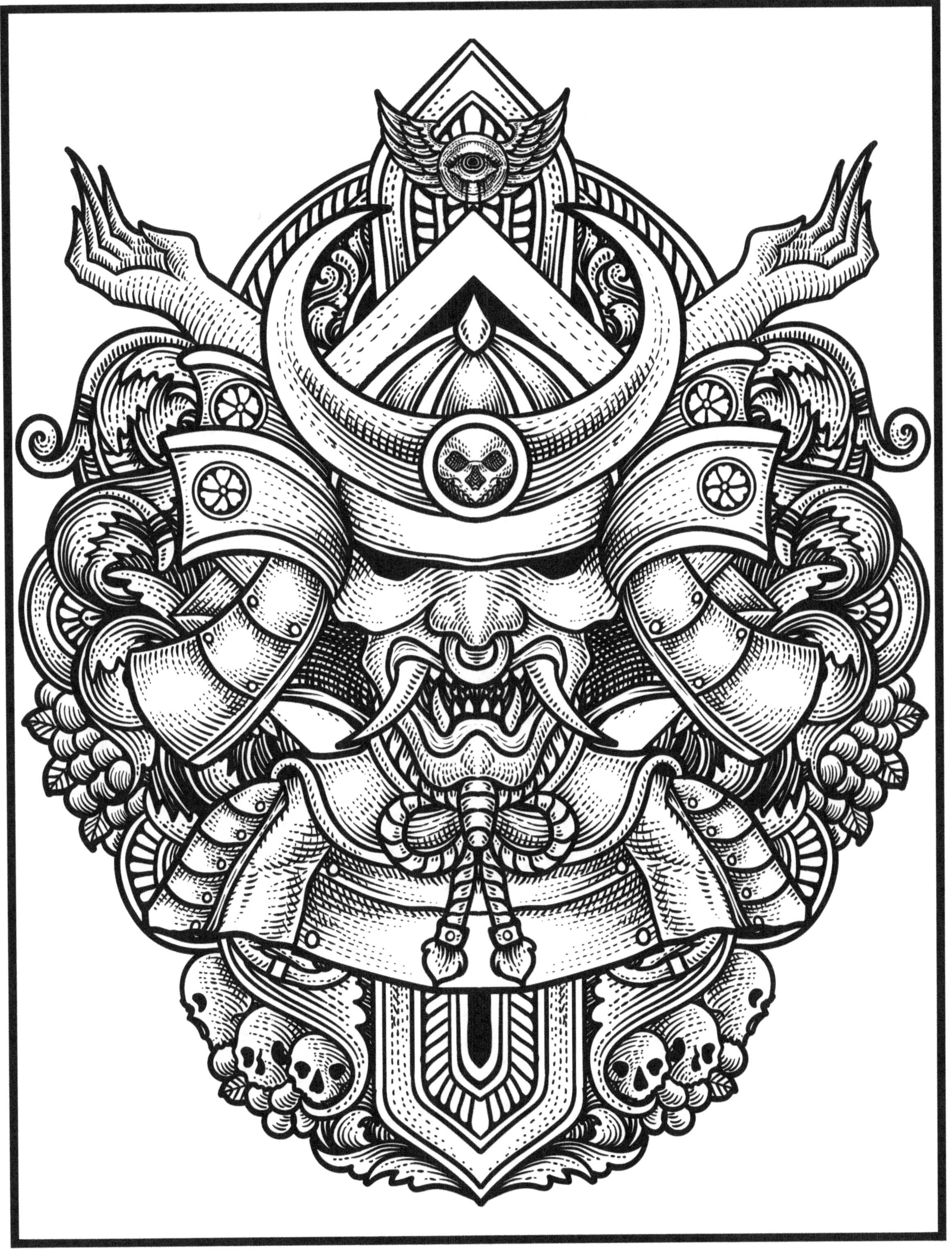

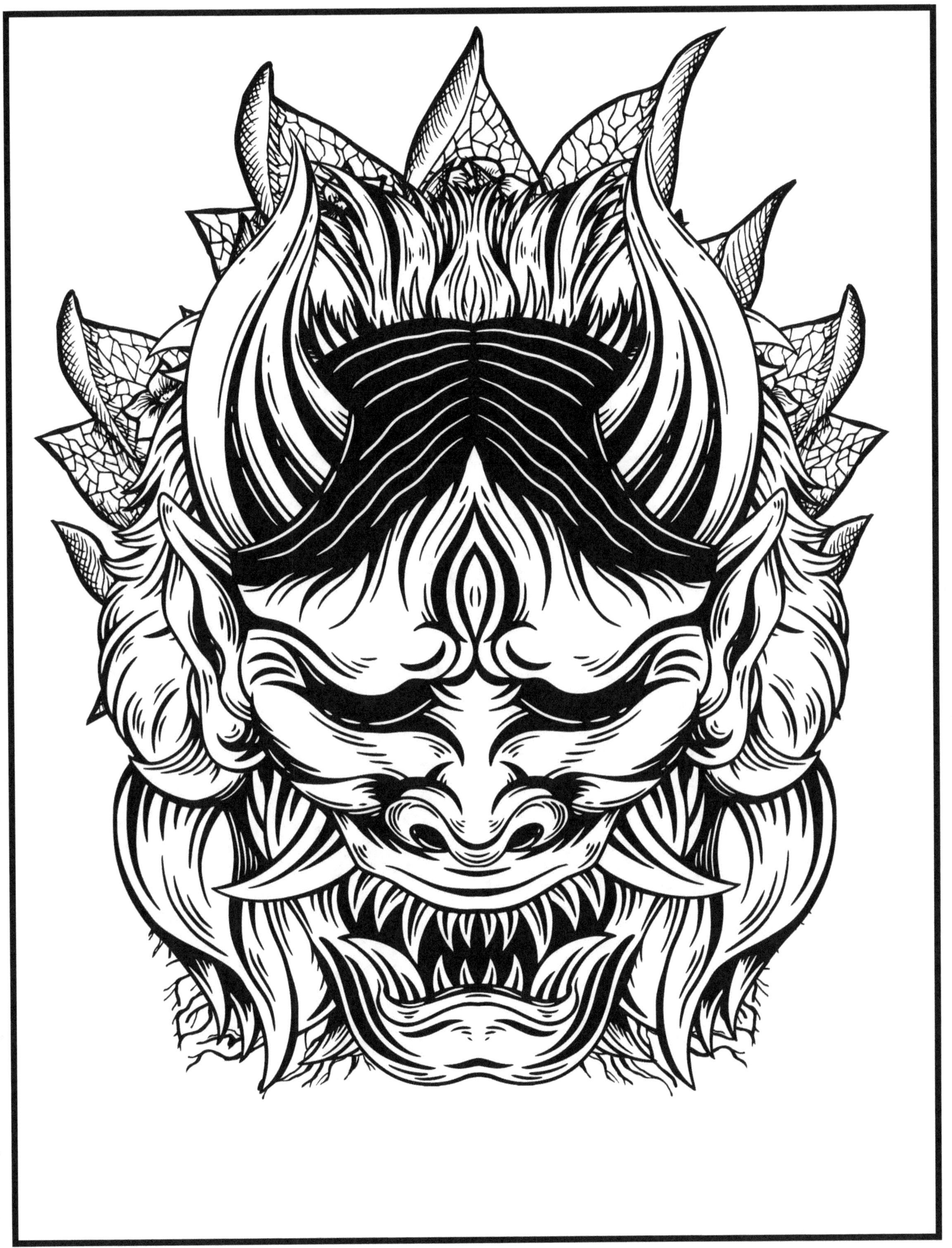

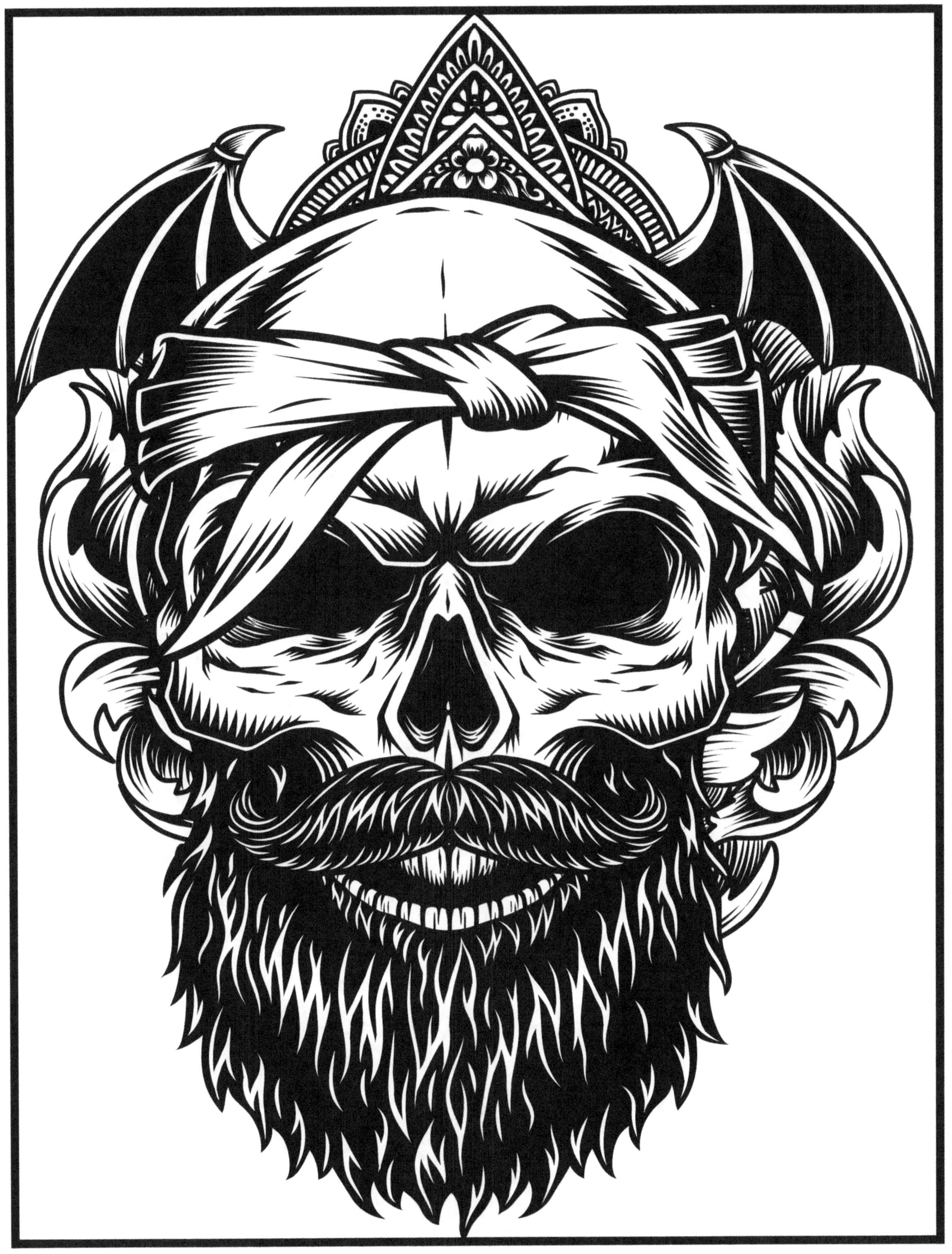

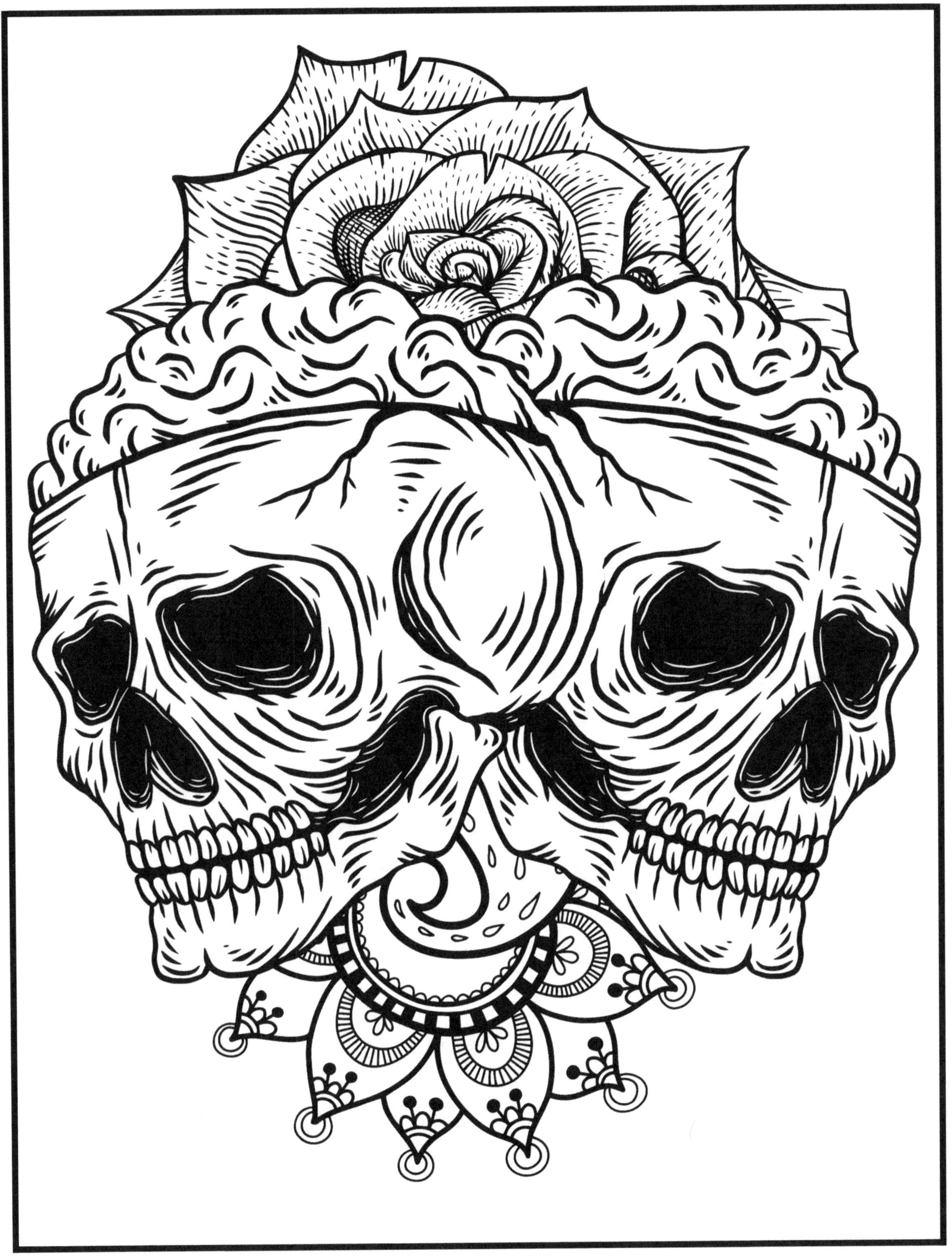

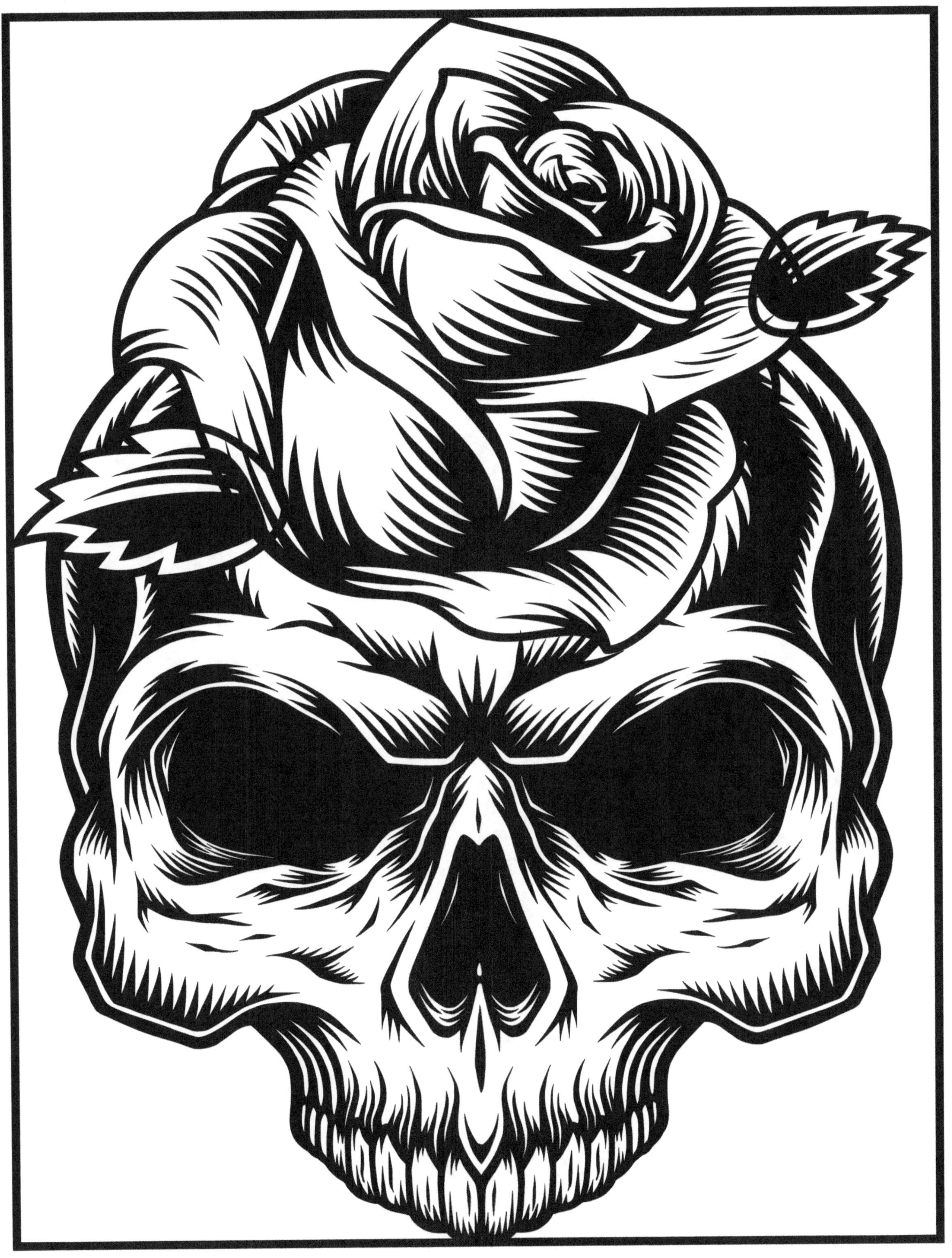

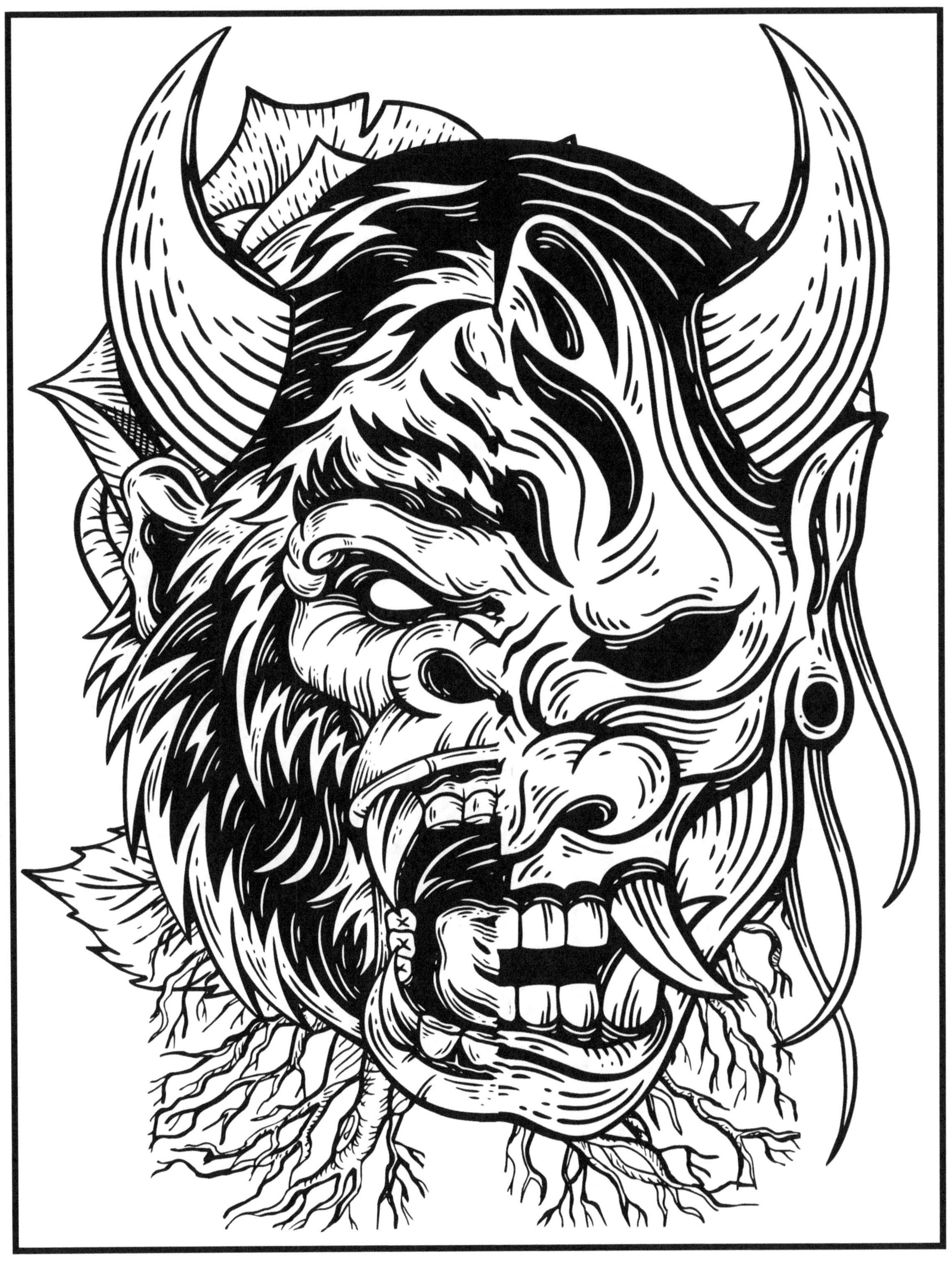

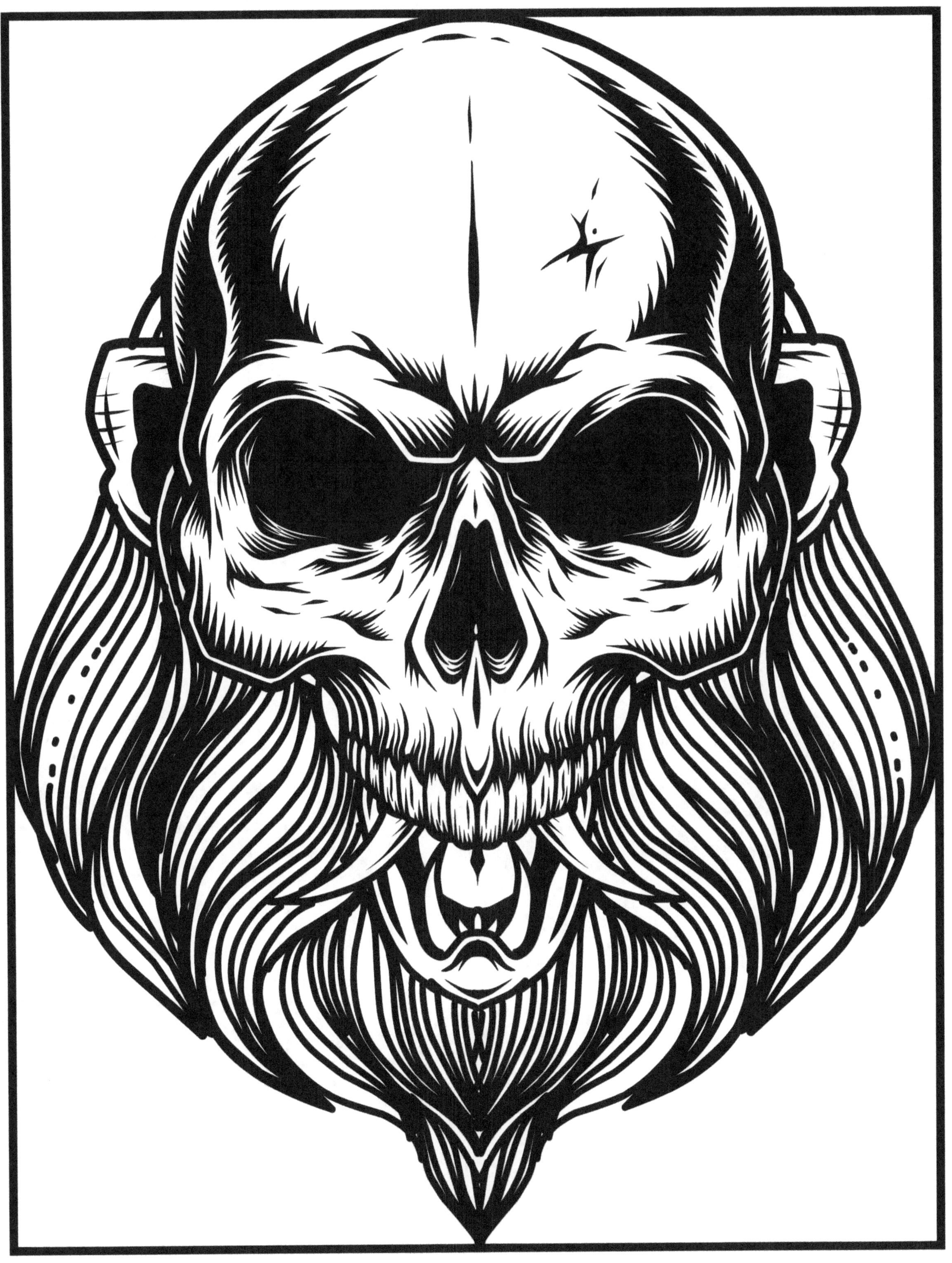

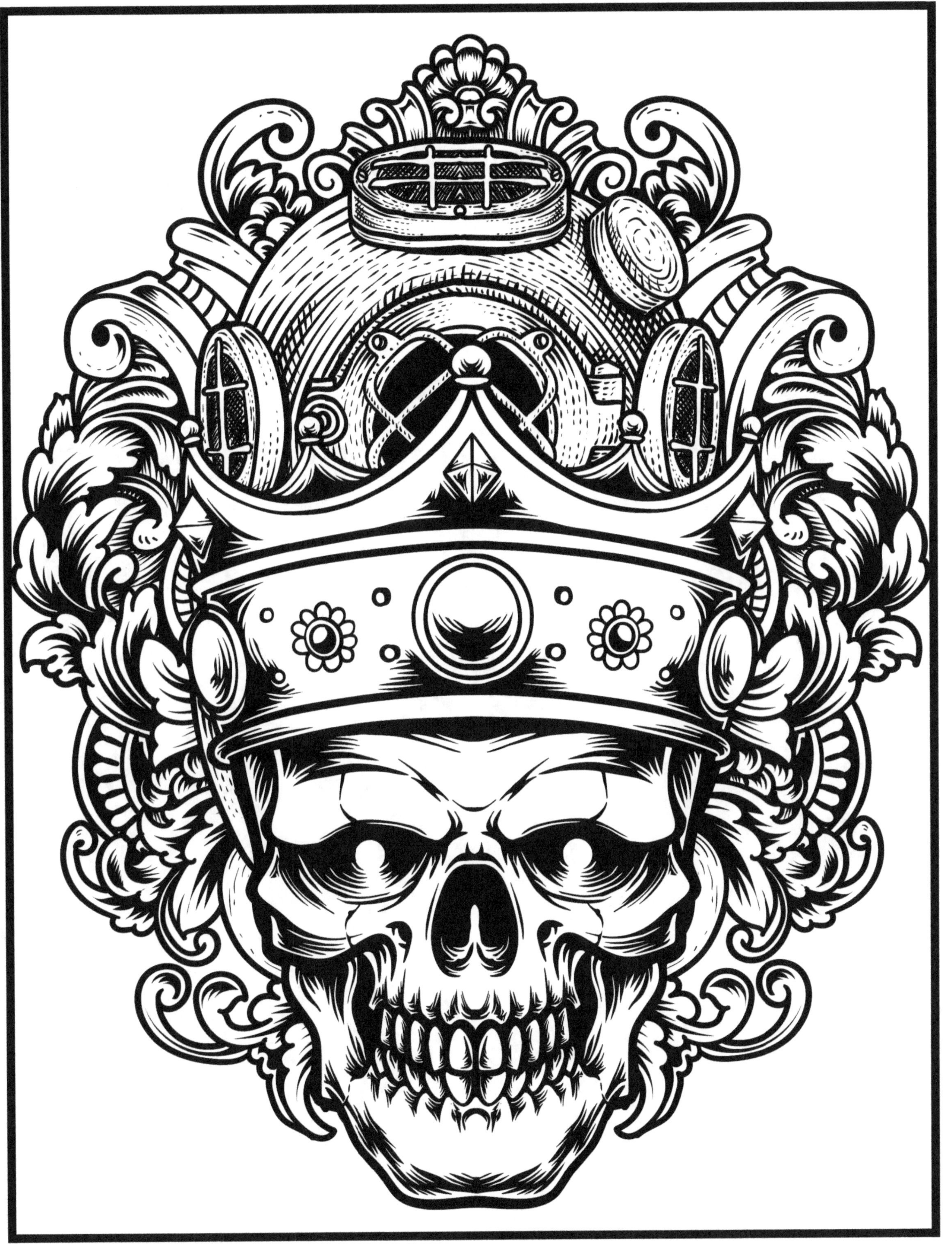

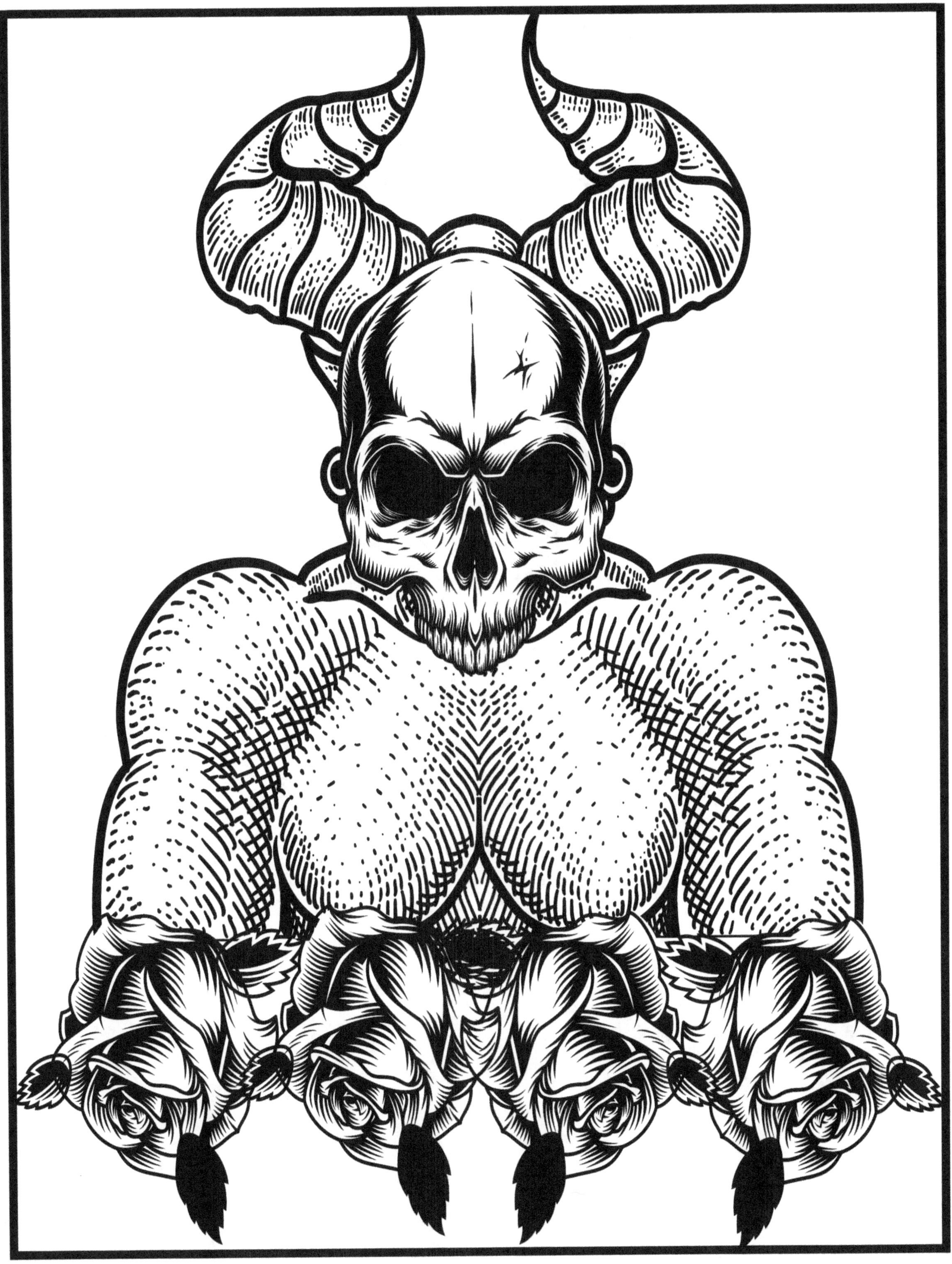

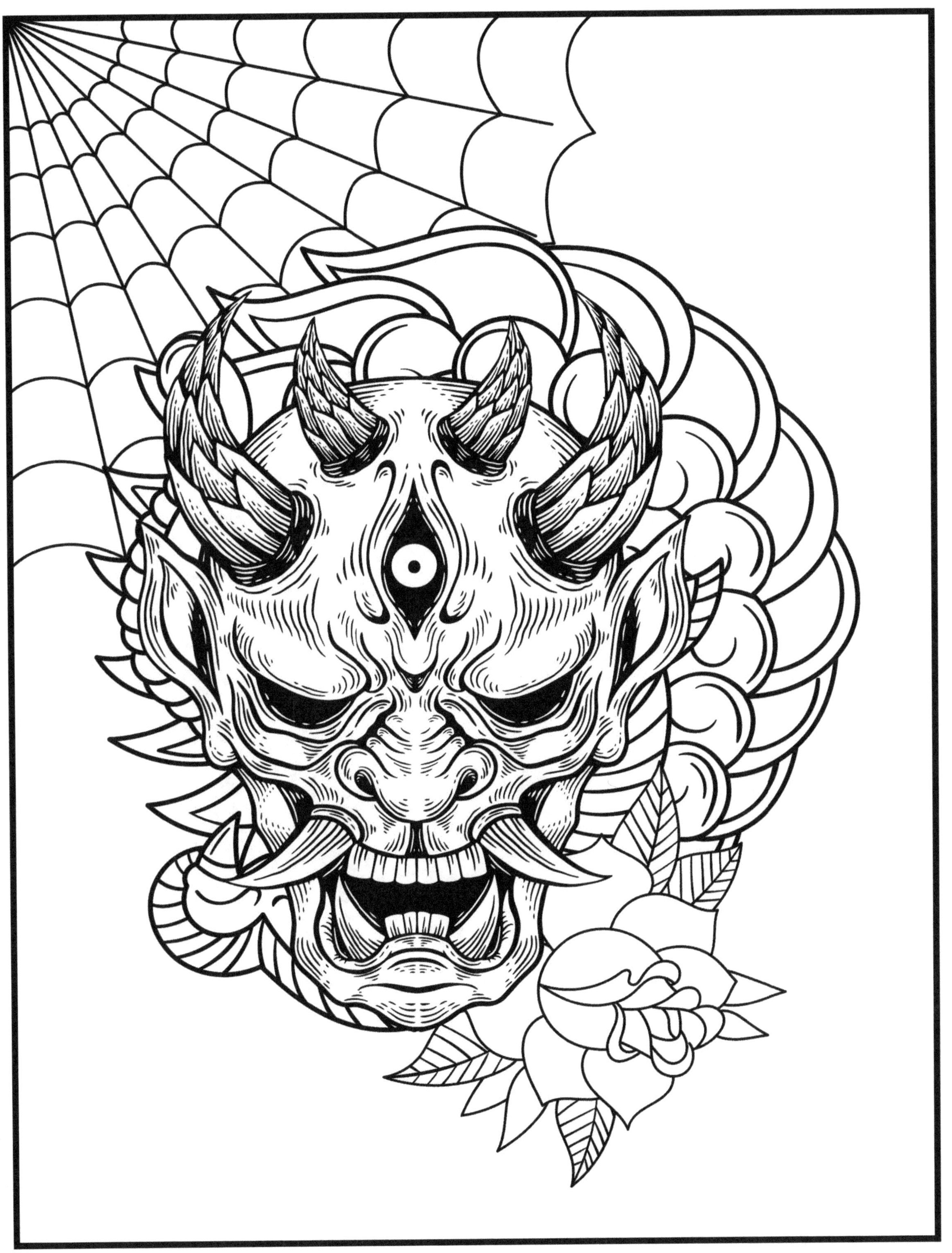

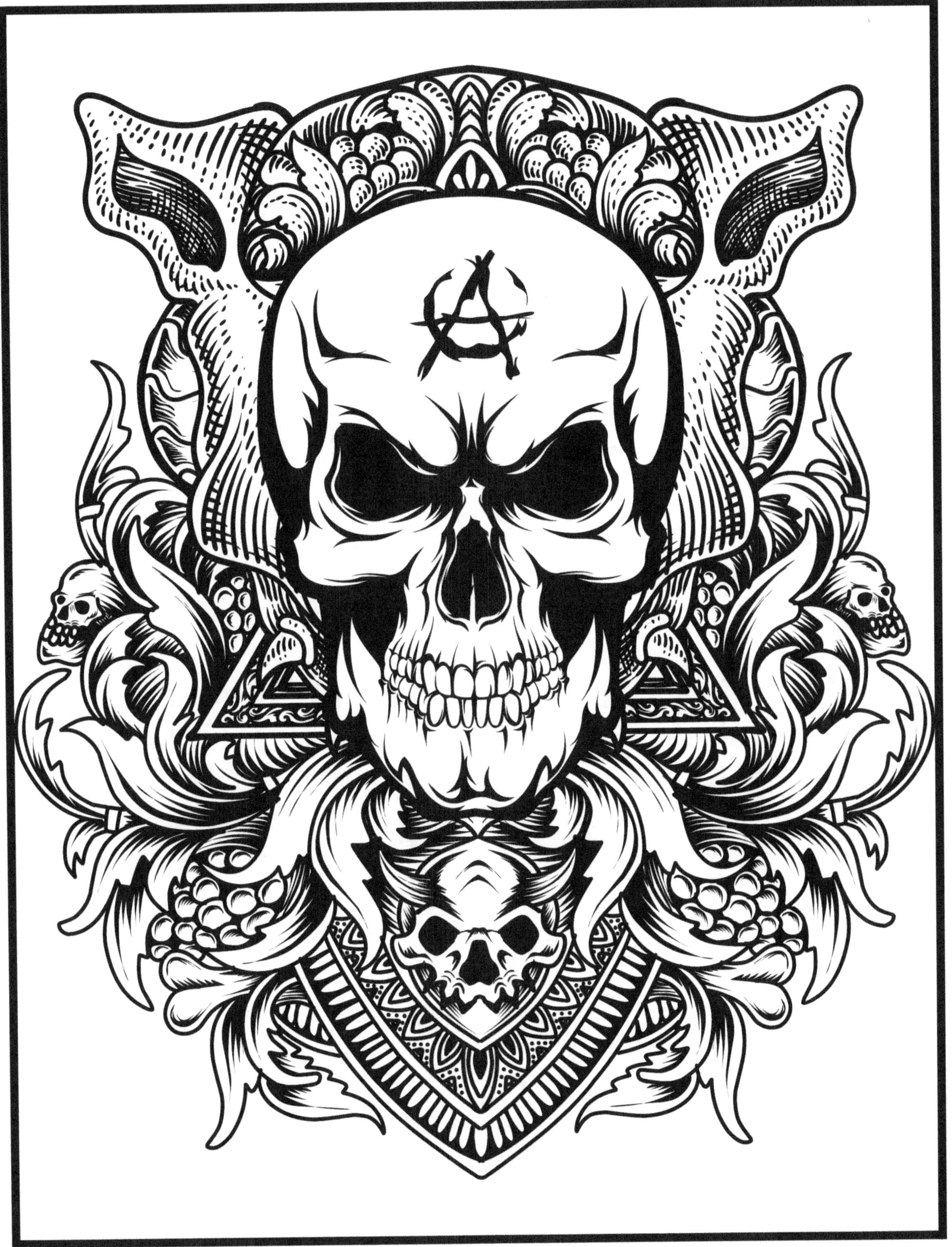

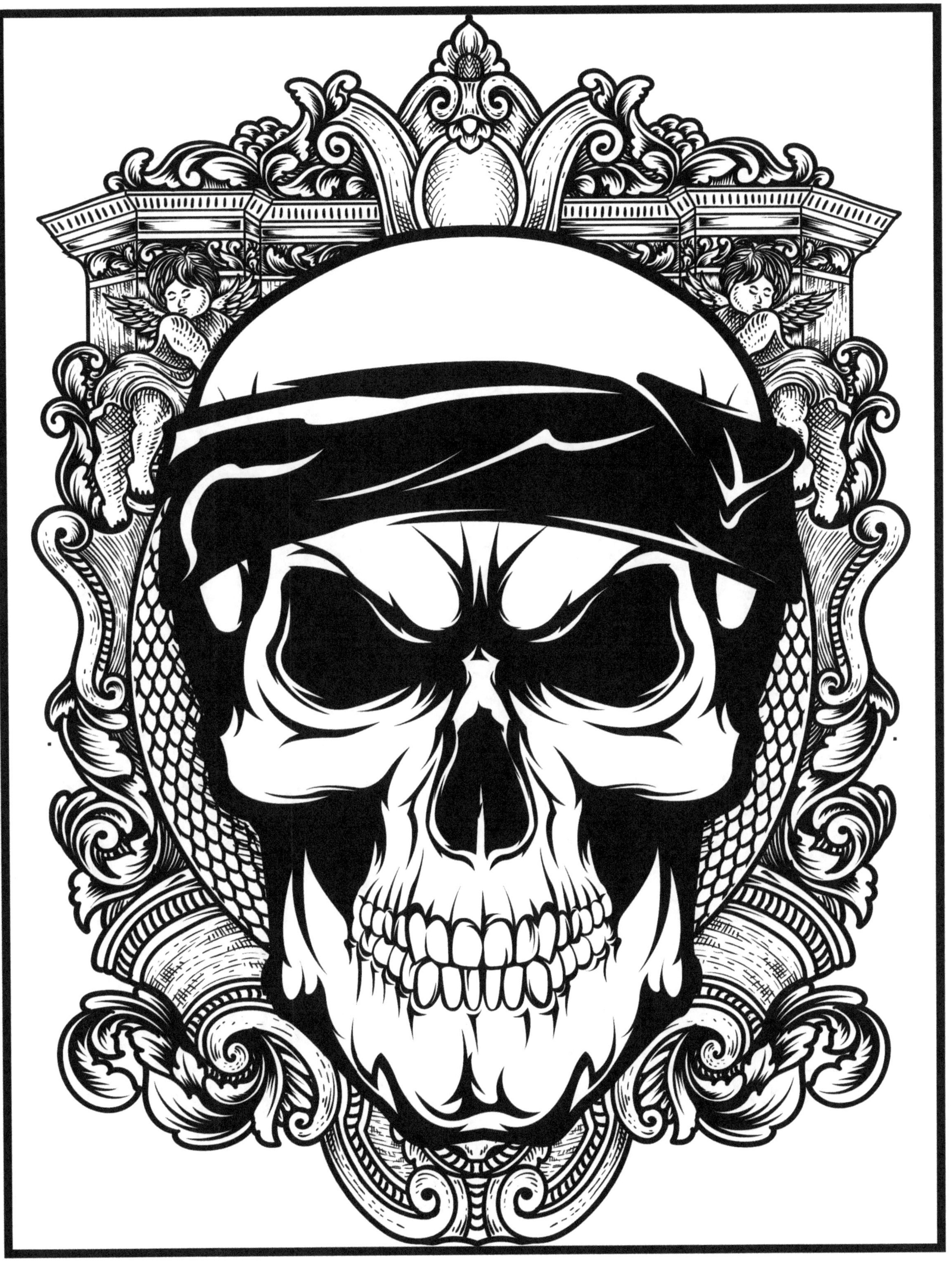

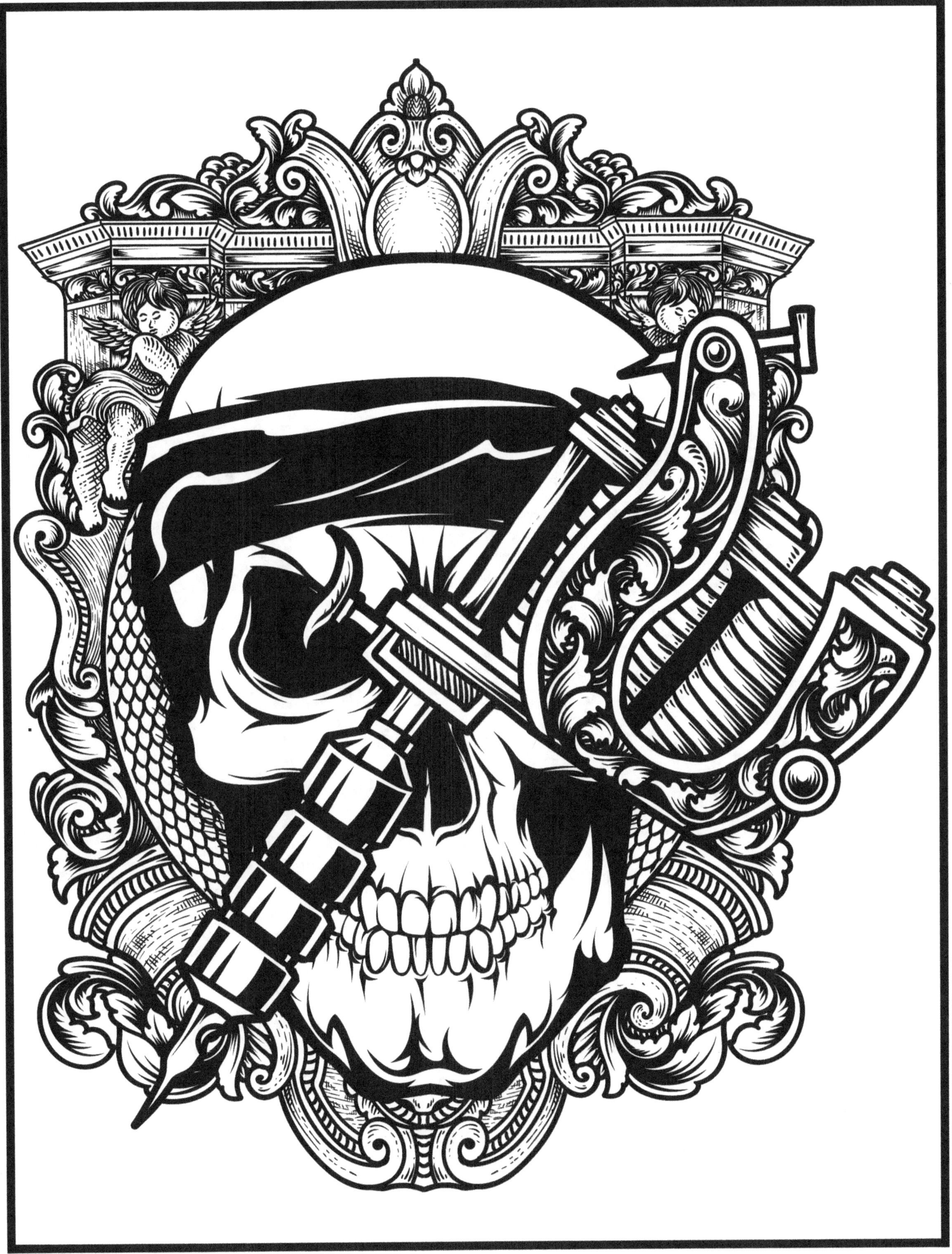

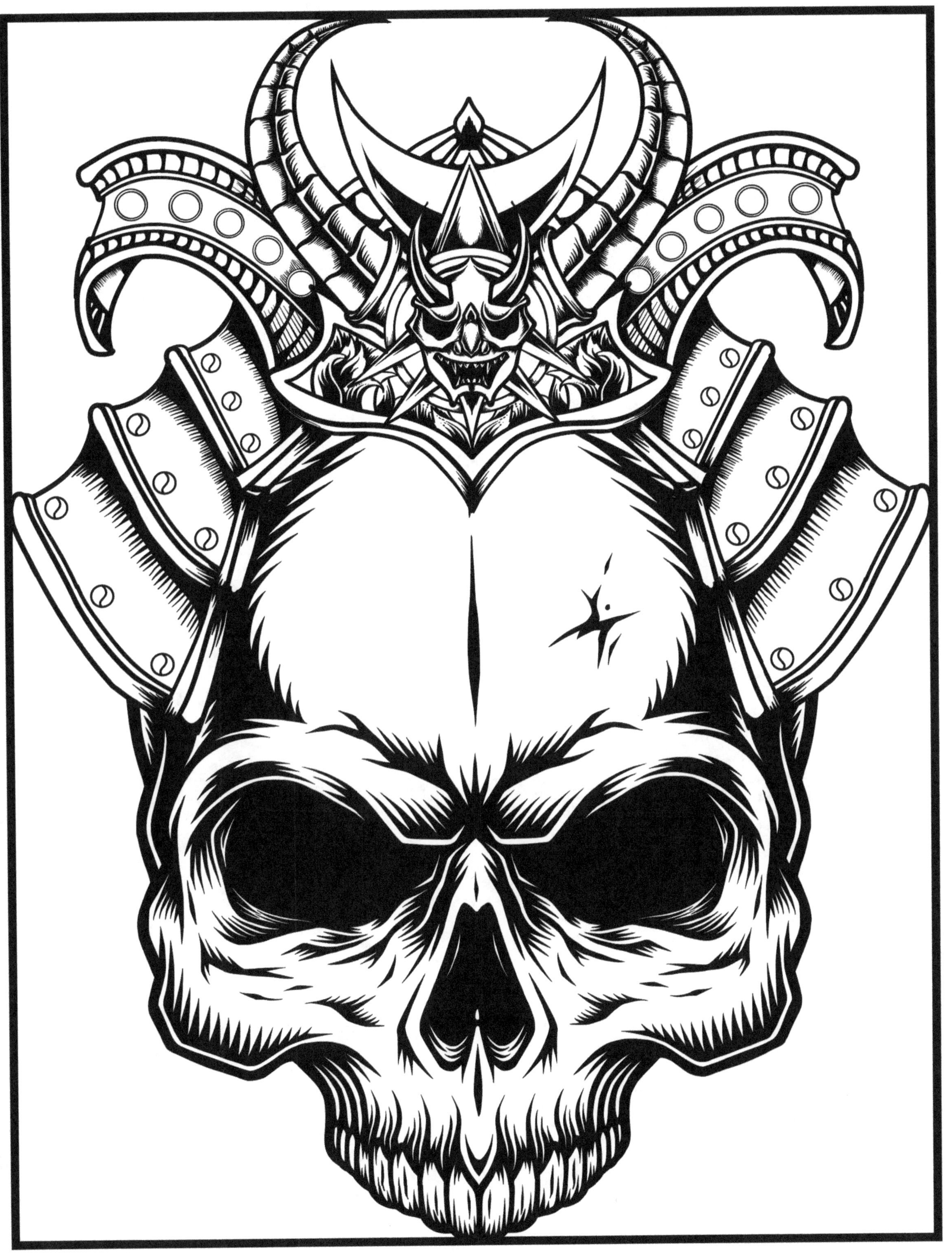

Thank you for colouring your way through
this delightful journey with
Brooks Brotherz colouring books!

We hope you've had a fantastic time
exploring our designs.

Your feedback means the world to us,
and we'd love to hear your thoughts.

If you enjoyed this coloring book,
please consider leaving a review on Amazon
to share your experience with others.

Your reviews help us continue creating
wonderful coloring adventures for everyone
to enjoy.

Thank you for your support,
and happy colouring!

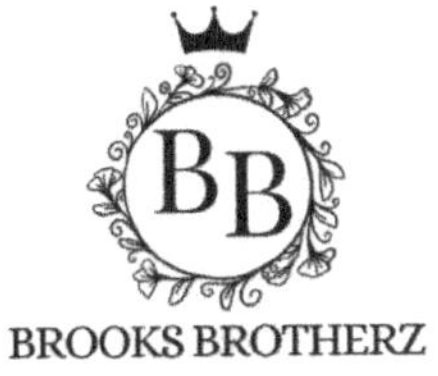